101 SIDE HUSTLES TO MAKE EXTRA MONEY

From Freelancing, Online Selling, Creative Gigs, Real Estate, Passive Income, At-Home Opportunities, and Many More!

Frank Jenkins

FREE BONUS

SCAN TO GET OUR NEXT BOOK FOR FREE!

TABLE OF CONTENTS

INTRODUCTION 1

1. DRIVE FOR LYFT OR UBER 5

2. DELIVER FOOD 7

3. DELIVER GROCERIES 8

4. BECOME A PHOTOGRAPHER.....................9

5. TUTOR ONLINE 10

6. BECOME A TRANSCRIPTIONIST..............12

7. TEACH LANGUAGES ONLINE 15

8. START AN AIRBNB BUSINESS...................16

9. SELLING ITEMS..18

10. START A DROP-SHIPPING BUSINESS ... 20

11. WHOLESALE REAL ESTATE 21

12. FREELANCING...22

13. AFFILIATE MARKETING 23

14. PRINT ON DEMAND....................................26

15. BLOGGING 28

16. CREATE AND SELL ONLINE COURSES. 30

17. PATREON 31

18. BECOME AN INSTAGRAM INFLUENCER33

19. RUN FACEBOOK   AND INSTAGRAM ADS FOR SMALL BUSINESSES...36

20. PROOFREAD FOR CONTENT WRITERS AND SMALL BUSINESSES 37

21. TAKE ONLINE SURVEYS 39

22. PINTEREST VIRTUAL ASSISTANT 42

23. SELL PRINTABLES ON ETSY 44

24. REFURBISH FURNITURE 46

25. WALK DOGS/PET SIT 47

26. RENT OUT YOUR CAR 49

27. HOUSE-SIT 51

28. GET CASH BACK WHILE SHOPPING..... 53

29. SHOPIFY.. 55

30. PLAY GAMES FOR CASH 56

31. COMPLETE TASKS ON TASKRABBIT..... 58

32. TEACH ART LESSONS................................ 60

33. RENT OUT YOUR POOL 63

34. BECOME A BOOKKEEPER........................ 65

35. CLEAN HOUSES 67

36. BECOME A SOCIAL MEDIA MANAGER 68

37. SELL SERVICES ON FIVERR...................... 69

38. FLIP CARS.. 70

39. SELL LESSON PLANS, CHEAT SHEETS, AND ACTIVITY SHEETS... 72

40. START A YOUTUBE CHANNEL 73

41. MOBILE AUTO DETAILING BUSINESS .. 75

42. INVEST IN REAL ESTATE 76

43. CHILDCARE SERVICES 77

44. LANDSCAPE 78

45. START A PODCAST 79

46. BECOME A MOBILE NOTARY 81

47. WATCH VIDEOS 82

48. SEWING 83

49. REVIEW AND WRITE RESUMES 84

50. REFEREE 85

51. CLINICAL RESEARCH TRIALS 86

52. ADVERTISE ON YOUR CAR 87

53. SELL OLD ELECTRONICS 89

54. PACKAGE DELIVERY DRIVER 90

55. GRAPHIC DESIGN 91

56. SOCIAL MEDIA AND SEARCH ENGINE RATER 92

57. AIRBNB EXPERIENCE HOST 93

58. WEDDING OFFICIANT 94

59. SELL CRAFTS 95

60. AT-HOME CLOTHES CLEANER 96

61. FLIP GOODS 97

62. COMPETITIVE GAMER 98

63. T-SHIRT DESIGNER 98

64. SELL PLASMA 99

65. FlexJobs 100

66. APPJOBS 101

67. SHIFTPIXY 102

68. WONOLO 103

69. USER INTERVIEWS 104

70. USER TESTING 104

71. RECRUITING 105

72. FASHION CONSULTANT 106

73. DRONE PILOT 106

74. PHOTO EDITING 107

75. TRANSLATE 108

76. CALL CENTER 109

77. CONTACT SERVICE AGENT 109

78. LOAN SIGNING AGENT 110

79. MATTRESS FLIPPING 111

80. MOVING SERVICES 111

81. MYSTERY SHOPPING 112

82. IN PERSON SMALL GIGS 113

83. STORAGE SERVICE 114

84. BECOME A MOVIE EXTRA 115

85. LOOK AT THINGS ON EBAY 116

86. CREATE PSYCHIC READINGS 117

87. SELL TAROT CARD READINGS 118

88. TALK TO PEOPLE ONLINE 119

89. CORPORATE GIFT CONSULTANT 119

90. PUBLIC SPEAKING COACH 121

91. HOLIDAY ERRAND SERVICE 121

92. DATING CONSULTANT 122

93. HOME FILMING LOCATION 123

94. PROCESS SERVER 123

95. VISUAL MERCHANDISER 124

96. SENIOR CITIZEN DOWNSIZING SERVICES
.... 125

97. UI/UX TESTER 126

98. DATA ENTRY 127

99. RECOVER UNCLAIMED PROPERTY 127

100. CRYPTO MINING 128

101. SOCIAL MEDIA ADVERTISING 129

CONCLUSION 131

INTRODUCTION

There was a time — a long time, in fact — when it seemed like everyone had a typical nine-to-five job. You would show up at your workplace, grab your timecard, clock in, and get started on your day. You worked hard from 9 AM to 5 PM, did your time, clocked out, drove home, and then spent time with your family.

For generations, Americans and people all over the world had a very concrete, time-tested idea of what a job looked like and how you were supposed to work it. Very rarely did people's experiences deviate from that typical schedule. Sure, some people worked in the food service industry, retail, or in various medical professions — they obviously kept different types of hours.

But for ages, most people felt that everyone should have one job and only one job, and they should have a reasonably structured, strict schedule for that job.

Well, times have changed drastically.

Over the last decade, the entire concept of what a job is and how you can make money has been transformed. Through the use of apps, internet sites, and web start-ups from all over the globe, lots of people are finding new, exciting, and innovative ways to earn a paycheck.

A major part of this new generation of workers and the places that employ them is the concept of the *side hustle*. Over the last few years, the side hustle has become helpful—and often downright essential—for millions of people, especially as the COVID-19 pandemic has taken hold and forced billions to change the way they see the world and how they work.

At one point, "side hustle" was considered an offensive term, or something that people would only speak of in hushed tones. Many were embarrassed to admit that they needed or desired an extra way to make money, a job that wasn't like a normal one. To some, it felt unreliable. To others, it felt desperate. There were many negative opinions about side hustles.

But that isn't the case anymore. The number of people who have turned to side hustles—and enjoy them—has exploded in the 21st century. In fact, as the COVID-19 pandemic raged on in the summer of 2021, it was estimated that one in three Americans had a side hustle. Although the impact of the pandemic eased in early 2022, many of those people continued with their side hustles instead of returning to more traditional jobs.

When working side hustles, people can choose the hours they want to work, sometimes alone and sometimes with others, in a format that doesn't feel rigid or structured. This allows the sort of work environment that so many people have sought for years yet didn't think was possible.

Via side hustles, workers are able to live normal lives and spend more time with friends and family, knowing they can pick up extra work when they have available time. Take Uber or DoorDash, for example. With these jobs, you can set your own hours and work when you want. You don't have to stick to a regimented schedule. This lets people still make money while also nurturing a healthy and happy life outside of work.

Side hustles are also allowing people to choose who they want to work with and when they want to be around people. These sorts of jobs let people operate by themselves far more than typical nine-to-five jobs do. Whether teaching online, running an Airbnb, selling items, or blogging, many side hustles don't require you to meet face-to-face with other people. Sometimes you never even see or speak with the person or company who is employing and paying you. For many people, this is a better way to work, and for years, it simply wasn't possible because today's opportunities didn't exist.

It is impossible to deny that America and the rest of the globe now live in a "gig economy." Are there dangers and problems that come along with that? Yes, there are. But there are also many benefits, especially for the working class. People can now supplement their income with jobs they are passionate about or replace their previous corporate hours with multiple gigs that leave their lives enriched rather than restricted. For millions of fortunate people, the days of clocking in and out are long gone. The exciting world of side hustles has arrived.

With so many choices, figuring out which gig is best for you may be difficult. If you type "side hustle" into a search engine, you will find millions of search results, and so many options can be downright overwhelming. But no matter what it is that drives you, fascinates you, and draws you in, there is a side hustle out there waiting.

In this book, you'll find a comprehensive list of the most profitable and exciting side hustle jobs available!

1.
DRIVE FOR
LYFT OR UBER

With the development and expansion of ridesharing systems, driving is becoming a trendy job. You've probably seen advertisements online and, more than likely, you've even used a ridesharing app yourself at some point. It's a great option if you are looking to choose your own hours and earn a living in the process. Plus, you get to have some fun conversations and sight-see simultaneously. Whether you have the option of driving for Uber, Lyft, or both will vary based on your location.

Both Lyft and Uber drivers operate in thousands of major cities throughout the globe and are even found in some smaller towns too. It's actually quite hard to find a U.S. city that doesn't have either or both of these side gigs available. Of course, you'll need a few items before you can start making money via ridesharing. You need to own a smartphone, a working driver's license, and a personal vehicle to use while driving. A background check is also required by both Uber and Lyft. In certain cities, a safety check of the vehicle is required. Depending on the city, you might need a business license.

The estimated profits for both services vary since you must account for your car's wear and tear, the mileage accumulated, the cost of fuel, and how often you will pick up passengers. Keep in mind that there are pockets of time spent waiting for customers to arrive at the curb. However, you might earn more money if you log on during a "surge pricing" period when vehicle trips are higher in demand.

There are a few downsides to ridesharing that you should keep in mind as well. For starters, many people hate sitting in traffic and, as you can imagine, that's a regular part of being an Uber or Lyft driver. You will be stuck behind other cars practically all day long, if you are working during rush hour or the "surge pricing" period. Will you get paid more? Of course, but your anxiety and stress levels might also suffer for it.

Additionally, if you are worried about germs, ridesharing might not be the right side hustle for you. At the height of the COVID-19 pandemic in 2020–2021, Uber and Lyft went to great lengths to ensure that every car was clean, and every driver and rider was safe. Those rules have eased since, but there is still a chance that you will be in close quarters with someone who is sick and could spread a virus or germs to you.

Sure, there are some issues that come along with driving for Uber and Lyft, and it's not for everyone. At the same time, it's also a great job that can pay an awful lot in just a short amount of time. Plus, you decide when you are open to taking rides and when you are not. This is an excellent side job to complement other forms of work.

2.
DELIVER FOOD

People aren't the only thing you can transport when you are pursuing driving as a side hustle. In fact, you can pick up and drop off food from restaurants all over your city and make some great money doing so.

It's true — one of the finest side businesses to bring in some extra money is food delivery using DoorDash. Since its launch in 2013, the platform has provided services to millions of users. DoorDash was pretty popular right when it launched, but it reached a new level of popularity and necessity during the COVID-19 pandemic when people were forced to order takeout from their local eateries. Not only did more people use DoorDash and its competitors during that time, but more people also started working for the delivery service.

That means that more people than ever before are relying on food delivery companies, not only for their yummy meals but also for their employment. So, you have plenty of chances to make money with apps like DoorDash.

If you choose to deliver food via DoorDash, you'll be compensated for the food you provide and for your service in the form of tips. Many people tip depending on several factors — how far you've traveled, the state of the food when it arrives, and your overall friendliness and attention to detail. Like any tipped job, providing good customer service will help you earn a little extra money in your pocket.

3.
DELIVER GROCERIES

Maybe you don't want to drive people or their restaurant food around. It's definitely not for everyone. If that's the case, you can deliver their groceries instead.

We all have to grocery shop, and through apps such as Instacart, you can now make some really good money doing it for other people. Nearly ten million Americans work for Instacart and have found it has many benefits, such as the ability to make their own schedule and the joy of working alone.

After selecting the items and having them bagged up, you will then drive to the customer's house and deliver the goods to their front step. It's a very straightforward — if a bit time-consuming — venture. There are some downsides. For example, there are often complications with an order. If someone requests a particular brand or item that isn't on sale, you'll have to make a substitution, which can cause some anxiety. Often, these conflicts are easily resolved without any issue. Additionally, you'll want to work hard to deliver the groceries quickly, especially if cold goods are involved. But most people think that working for Instacart is a lot of fun, despite these possible hang-ups.

There are now multiple apps that you can use to become a grocery delivery professional. It's not just Instacart. Postmates, Shipt, and Amazon Prime Now are all examples of newly created apps that allow you to shop for other people and get paid handsomely to do so.

4.
BECOME
A PHOTOGRAPHER

If you have a passion and natural eye for creating art, you could become a photographer and make some serious cash doing so.

There are many reasons people might need photographers. They are called upon for weddings, parties, graduations, and a slew of other events. And there are two things that everyone needs when they are looking for someone to take photos for them: a good price and a good product. Can you deliver both?

Make sure to you ask anyone who hires you if you can use some of the photos you take to advertise your business. You don't want to use them without permission.

Remember, there are other ways that you can make money with your camera without doing paid gigs. You can sell stock photos on services like Shutterstock or Foap. You do this by creating an account and uploading a portfolio of your work.

No matter how you use your photography skills for money-making, you should practice before you get out there. Remember that it may take some time before you make serious money from photography. It doesn't happen overnight. But unlike some of the other jobs mentioned in this book, this is one that can pay very handsomely per hour once you've put in the work to build your business.

5.
TUTOR ONLINE

It's time you put your good education to work!

Were you the student who did a great job teaching others? If so, tutoring could be the right approach for you to make some extra money. Indeed, tutoring is the sort of side hustle that is making many people a lot of money, and the best part about it is that there is *always* a need for a tutor somewhere.

We all know how tutoring works. You will meet with a student and focus on a subject they're having trouble with. It may be English, Math, Science, or something else. For this job, it is ideal to have a higher level of education than the students you are teaching. For example, it's recommended you have a bachelor's degree in English before helping first-year college students with their term papers. However, even if you are only a high school student, you could still help grade-level children develop their basic math skills.

Finding someone to tutor is a little difficult at times. Many people turn to sites such as Craigslist, Facebook, or NextDoor to create ads and find potential clients. That's a great approach, but there are other options too. Whatever approach you take, make sure it looks professional. Remember that the clientele you'll be attracting are mostly parents, and they will not be willing to spend money on someone who doesn't seem to know what they're doing.

In addition to posting ads yourself, you can teach online through websites such as Lever.co, SuperProf, TutorMe, and Tutors. These websites are helpful because they will aid in matching you up with the right students. The only downside with this route is that you will need to go through an application process before starting to work.

6.
BECOME A
TRANSCRIPTIONIST

You might not be aware of the role of a transcriptionist, but it's a job that is needed in many different industries, and it's one that you can do from home!

Becoming a transcriptionist means that you'll be converting audio or video files into written formats. You'll listen to or watch something and then type out *exactly* what was said. Obviously, this side hustle is great for someone who has superior listening skills. If you aren't able to do this job in a quiet space that doesn't have many distractions, you should probably avoid it. That is because anything less than pure perfection with your transcriptions simply cannot be tolerated.

The solitude of operating alone and the lack of dealing with incoming calls or complaints of dissatisfied clients are additional pros for those who work in their own home offices as a transcriptionist. In other words, this side hustle creates a great sense of freedom. If you follow this career path for your side hustle, you may also learn something new and intriguing based on what you're listening to and writing down.

Transcriptionists come in a variety of forms. The transcribing market is typically divided into three subsectors: general, medical, and legal.

A license from your state or perhaps the completion of a certification program is probably necessary to work as a transcriptionist who focuses on medical or legal transcription. You'll also need the ability to comprehend complex legal or medical jargon. Compared to ordinary transcribing labor, these specialist sectors frequently pay more. But remember that accuracy is even more important in these fields. Remember, perfection isn't just preferred — it's required.

The text for a range of video or audio files is provided by general transcriptionists. You could transcribe podcasts or conversations for a writer or blogger. You might record corporate meetings, university classes, conference presentations, and talks held during focus groups for marketing.

Additionally, broadcast captioners provide closed captions. You have seen closed captions many times, and they are always written by transcriptionists worldwide. In fact, there's a considerable demand for captioning written in real-time, specifically for live events or broadcasts, and it often pays more money. But it's a bit more high-stakes and fast-paced. Imagine watching a live TV show and writing down what the people on the screen are saying at their pace. As you can guess, it can end up being a bit stressful.

Medical experts such as doctors speak on audio recordings, which medical transcriptionists then turn into official, written reports. Medical transcriptionists can work from home but can also be found in clinics, hospitals, laboratories, ORs, and other medical facilities.

Based on the firm you work for and the jobs you take on, functioning as a medical transcriptionist may require a license, qualification, or prior work experience. You'll require a solid grasp of medical jargon, anatomy, processes, and recording of healthcare.

Although working as a medical transcriptionist can be more lucrative than working as a general online transcriptionist, the Bureau of Labor Statistics predicts a 3% job loss in this industry over the next ten years. This drop is being caused by technological developments, such as the usage of voice recognition software and outsourcing to other countries.

Legal recorders produce textual transcripts of depositions, trials, and other legal procedures. A typical kind of legal transcriptionist is a court reporter.

Legal transcriptionists are also engaged to transcribe recordings of undercover law enforcement, victim interviews, and police interrogations. The written materials they provide are frequently utilized to aid attorneys in trial preparation and could be relied upon in a court of law.

A qualification or license is typically needed for people who provide legal transcription services. Although there is some work on-site in courtrooms, legislative sessions, law firms, and other legal settings — many legal transcriptionists operate virtually.

Prices under $50 per audio hour are thought to be too low by seasoned transcriptionists, but you may earn $9 to $10 per hour if you are just starting out. You can find entry-level transcription jobs using search engines or freelance websites, which are covered later in this book.

7.
TEACH LANGUAGES ONLINE

If you are someone with a strong handle on the English language, then there may be a slew of side hustles waiting for you. Teaching someone else English is an easy, profitable way to tackle a side hustle that is second nature to you.

Many people all over the world want to learn English. Because of the internet, they can do this online with ease.

Many English teachers create lesson plans and have meetings, classes, and tests, all via webcam.

Here is something you should definitely keep in mind when you are hoping to find a job teaching English: have you ever taught anything before? Being a teacher isn't as easy as you might think. You really need to take a step back and figure out how to break down the lessons you want to relay to your students. Remember, you will teach things you've known for decades. How often do you think about how you talk and why you talk that way? You will need to get into the nitty-gritty of the English language—how it works, and *why* it works that way—when you are teaching English.

8.
START AN
AIRBNB BUSINESS

Airbnb is increasingly being used by tourists as a fun, convenient alternative when traveling. They are sick and tired of hotels, motels, and the hassles that come with them. Some tourists seek a sense of familiarity when they are away from home. Others are seeking lodgings that can house large groups of people in one location. In addition, many people consider short-term, peer-to-peer rentals to be less expensive than traditional hotel rooms. If you're considering joining the trend and renting out a room, you may end up making your side business your primary source of income.

You can choose when and how much to charge for your living space. You can list for free and can personally approve guests. Take a look at rival listings to determine the asking price in your neighborhood before selecting your pricing. You should take into account the expenses associated with hosting, such as cleaning, higher electricity bills, taxes, and Airbnb's host charge of 3% for handling payments. Airbnb charges six to twelve percent in booking fees from your visitors. Make sure you are familiar with Airbnb's host requirements, including those for listing accuracy, communicating with visitors, honoring reservation promises, cleaning your home for each visitor, and offering essentials like soap and toilet paper.

Although you are not likely to risk physical harm when you rent out your home, consider safeguarding your valuables. Most Airbnb hosts prepare ahead of time by creating a secure location to lock up their valuable photo albums, jewelry, and documents. You can protect yourself by securing a portion of the house, such as a hall closet, or maybe bar the garage from guest use completely. Don't offer visitors a chance to take your belongings or your identity.

If you continue to live in your house while renting out a portion of it, things can grow more complicated. You may be able to keep a closer eye on your belongings, but if your guest ends up being harmful, you are physically exposed. Running criminal background checks on visitors before they make a reservation or before they arrive is unrealistic—you can use the internet to conduct basic research, but it's not foolproof.

You can always refuse an Airbnb guest or even cancel the booking. However, in some circumstances, Airbnb will charge a fee. Reviews from past hosts can also give you peace of mind. You can choose to only accept reservations from those who have successfully gone through Airbnb's Verified ID procedure. Through the uploading of a legitimate government-issued ID and the linking of a Facebook account to an Airbnb account, both hosts and guests can have Airbnb verify their identification.

9.
SELLING ITEMS

Today, many online options make it easy to sell and resell items. Amazon Prime was introduced in February 2005 and is one of the easiest and most popular routes for selling goods.

According to research, 50% of all third-party merchants use Amazon FBA. At the same time, 75% of the biggest Amazon merchants trust Amazon with handling their order fulfillment. The fact that so many people utilize this service demonstrates how beneficial and practical it is.

You can use Amazon's resources to run your business, including its employees and facilities, as well as its experience and recognized expertise. When looking into this option, keep in mind that you will need a few things before getting started. Amazon will require an application process in which your products will need approval, and a video interview will take place to confirm your identity. In addition to this, it is a good idea to create an inventory. You can start this process by using companies such as Printful or Printify, which have helpful step-by-step video tutorials available online. Another thing to keep in mind is that there is a fee to sign up. If this is sounding a little too large scale for you, selling stuff through Amazon isn't your only option.

Another great online opportunity is eBay, which offers an opportunity to sell new and used goods. Although eBay started as an online auction site for secondhand goods and collectibles, it gradually changed to a fixed-price site. It's now a fantastic location to market recently released goods as well. The fact that anybody can quickly create a seller account and begin selling on eBay accounts for the millions of vendors who use the site today.

Getting started as an eBay seller is very simple. In one day, you can open your account, put up a product for sale, and then find a buyer for it. Selling any outdated items you have laying around your home on eBay may be a quick and profitable method to get rid of them.

The number of triumphs you experience on eBay depends on you. What began as a decluttering project could very well develop into a dependable side business or perhaps even entirely replace your existing income.

The procedure for selling on eBay is straightforward: the seller posts the item, the buyer makes the transaction, and the order is completed.

You can start small while selling on eBay, which is a terrific perk. Even if there is nothing you want to sell around your home, you can also sell family recipes and the like, which is a good way to build your seller reputation without spending any money at all.

10.
START A
DROP-SHIPPING BUSINESS

The order-fulfillment technique known as drop-shipping enables business operators to sell straight to customers without maintaining an inventory. A third-party provider sends a customer's order of goods from a drop-shipping company directly. The consumer pays the retail price you decide on, and you pay the suppliers' wholesale price. The remaining amount is profit. The best thing about drop-shipping is that you never deal with goods or spend money on stock.

Through a company like AliExpress, you can purchase millions of items from the drop-shipping marketplace and import them instantly into your store.

When a consumer makes a purchase in an online marketplace, the drop-shipping company automatically completes the order. Simply double-check the accuracy of the order data before sending the order through. The goods are subsequently delivered to the buyer, wherever they may be on the globe, by the AliExpress drop-shipping provider or any other company you rely on.

11.
WHOLESALE
REAL ESTATE

You may not be very well acquainted with the ins and outs of the real estate market, but you don't need to be if you want to be a wholesale real estate agent.

The entire concept is easy to follow. It's all about connecting the right people and then experiencing the sweet profit. When pursuing wholesale real estate, you are simply finding people with homes that need to be sold and then connecting those people with house flippers. But here's where you make your money—you charge a "finder's fee" for finding the home.

Think of it this way: If someone wants to sell a home for $250,000, you tack on another $10,000 for an assignment fee and then sell the package to the right house flipper. The homeowner gets the $250,000, and you get the $10,000 on top of that.

Getting into wholesale real estate is all about knowing how much a house sells for and how much house flippers are willing to spend. It's about communicating with the right parties, making connections, and staying tuned in to the real estate industry. It will require a lot of research and understanding of the complicated world of real estate, but, as you can tell, it could be worth it. This side hustle pays well and is worth the investment of knowledge and time!

12.
FREELANCING

Freelancers provide a variety of services for individual people as well as companies. If you want to be a freelancer, you can be someone who writes, reads, edits, draws, paints, records their voice, or any number of things. Practically any sort of job can be found through freelancing. Although this job may lack the security that comes with promised hours from a company, it has the potential pay just as well as a traditional job without the strings and confinements of one.

So, if you're looking to do freelance work, how do you find clients who will hire you? That's easy! Multiple websites, such as UpWork, Freelancer, Fiverr, and more, allow you to build a freelance profile, reach out to employers, and make the connections needed to land jobs. You'll have to create a portfolio of your previous work in order to find clients, and you'll need to make sure you sell yourself well. But no matter what sort of freelance work you want to tackle, these websites can help you make your side hustle dream a reality.

13.
AFFILIATE MARKETING

Affiliate marketing is when an individual makes money from promoting the goods of another individual or business. The affiliate merely looks for an item they are interested in and then promotes it and receives either free products or a commission based on sales.

Affiliate marketing utilizes the skills of a range of people for a more successful marketing approach while giving contributors a piece of the profit since it works by dividing the responsibility of product promotion and production between parties. Three parties must cooperate for this marketing method to succeed:

- The sellers of the goods
- The advertiser
- The customer

The seller is a merchant or perhaps a creator, whether they are a sole proprietor or a multinational corporation. A tangible item like domestic products or a service like cosmetics instructions may both be considered the product.

This is an ideal option for people who have active social media profiles with a large following. If there are any products or services you are already using, it is a good idea to message the providers/sellers and inquire whether they have an affiliate program. Sometimes they will give you sample products, and other times you will receive a special coupon code for your followers to use.

If you receive free products, often you are then required to post pictures, reels, or videos on your social media accounts featuring those products. This is great for getting free snacks, furniture, clothing, etc. It is highly recommended to choose products you already use and know you like so that your promotions are honest.

If you choose to receive affiliate codes, these are great for services and products you are already actively using. For example, as a writer, there are specific pens I prefer and purchase regularly, and there are programs I am subscribed to for my work and internet security. These are all great places to start when reaching out to companies for affiliate marketing opportunities. It is easy for me to post a photo of myself writing with the pens that I'm already loyal to or to write a blog post about why I choose specific programs and include my special code. These special codes often provide a discount for the products you are promoting and a commission for anything bought with the code. To get started with this gig, simply look up the products you commonly use and send those companies an e-mail asking if they have any affiliate marketing programs, making sure to tell them how many followers you have across your accounts.

In addition to using these methods, there are also plenty of websites that are designed for affiliate marketing. A good example is Clickfunnels.com which will pay you 40% of monthly commissions for each user you bring in. There is a cost to sign up for this, but it can be quite lucrative if you have an audience on any social media platform. Other websites include Bluehost and Amazon Associates. Most VPN services will also pay people to promote their products. For these websites the key is to find products with high conversion rates (lots of people buy when they visit the page) and high commission rates.

14.
PRINT
ON DEMAND

There are many websites out there that allow you to design products and then have those products made as they are purchased. This is called print-on-demand or POD. With this method, the price the customer pays for your products will be higher, but you will not have to keep an inventory in your home or garage.

The suppliers have what are known as "white label" items. These are things like blank coffee mugs and t-shirts just waiting for your design to be printed on them for sale. If you don't have a text idea or logo already in your pocket, you can often find design templates through the host websites.

For most sites, you'll sign up for a small fee and then place a payment method on file. Designing your products is free. After you create unique products, you'll want to list them on your website and link your website to your POD shop. Customers will pay you through your listed website (whether it's personal or something such as an Etsy or

Instagram shop), and the order will be sent to the POD shop to fulfill. You will want to have some money saved up, as these entities charge you separately. Often, the POD shop charges your account wholesale prices, creates your item, and ships it, while your personal shop will charge your customer retail prices, and that money will deposit in your account. To avoid any kind of issues, it is best to have reserve funds set up in case one transaction goes through faster than the other.

When developing products and product prices, it is recommended to conduct research. You'll have to decide whether to include shipping in your listed product price or not. Making this decision can be frustrating, especially if you want to offer shipping internationally. For example, a mug might cost you $5 wholesale, but then cost $6 shipping to one location and $12 shipping to another. If you wanted to offer free shipping (which could be a good marketing tactic), you would want to price the mug so that it will cover shipping costs regardless of destination and still earn a profit. This will also apply to providing items of multiple sizes and colors (such as t-shirts) since some colors or sizes may cost more to create.

Some people may choose to price things differently if they know they will not sell many of a certain item. For example, maybe they only earn fifty cents on every one of their 2XL shirts sold, but they gain a 300% profit on all of their small and medium shirts, and more people are purchasing their t-shirts because of the free shipping. It would be better to have all of these items cost the same and just take the hit for the larger shirts than to be greedy and possibly lose customers due to a price increase on larger garments.

Ultimately, these pricing decisions will come down to personal preference and strategy. It's highly recommended to watch videos and read articles about how other people are pricing items on the same platforms that you're using.

This is a great way to start a shop because the start-up cost is low, and you don't have to purchase your inventory before it's sold to customers. You'll just pay the sign-up fee and then the print-on-demand company handles the rest from there. Some examples of places to start include Tee Spring, merch by Amazon, KDP, Redbubble, Shopify, Printify, and Printful.

15.
BLOGGING

Blogging is a lot of fun! In fact, you have probably already written or read at least one blog at some point in your life. But did you know that blogging could become a side hustle that pays you handsomely?

Indeed, blogging is a great way to make money, but it takes time. It starts with an idea. You need to figure out what sort of blog you want to run. What fascinates you? What subjects do you have a lot of knowledge about? In other words, what is something that you can write about often, with expertise and a unique voice, and in ways that will attract a reading audience?

Then you need to start your blog and write consistently. And you'll need to find an audience. This can be done by creating a Facebook or social media page, reaching out to other blogs, or even advertising on other sites. But it's vital that you find people who will read your page regularly because that is the key to making some money.

The way to turn blogging into a proper side hustle is via advertising. Through Google as well as other sites and companies that provide ads, you will be able to post advertisements on your blog. But this will only pay off after you've established a reliable audience. Therefore, it's very important to ensure you are writing well and in a way that brings in readers.

Aside from having your own blog, you can also sell blog writing services to other companies. This is a good way to write about many different subjects that interest you. You can find clients through social media advertising, creating a personal website, or freelance websites like the ones mentioned earlier in this book. I have written for companies such as coffee roasteries that wanted regular articles about coffee and various products (they were actually affiliate marketing). I was hired through a freelance company and paid hourly. Some weeks I would only write a single article, and other weeks I would write as many as ten articles, depending on my time constraints and motivation.

16.
CREATE AND SELL ONLINE COURSES

Are you ready to be a teacher? If you are, you may have found the side hustle of your dreams. This might seem a little intimidating at first, but I promise you don't have to be an expert to share your knowledge. Passion goes a long way, and there are tons of ways you can sell what you know regardless of your skill level. For example, if you know how to play guitar — maybe you are not at the Santana level and more at the "Stairway to Heaven" level of expertise. That's okay. There are kids who would love to learn those basics, and they will pay to see what you have to show them.

Your choice of subject is completely up to you. It might be anything from website design to baking or relationship advice. What matters is that it's something you're excited and knowledgeable about because that is what makes an online course successful.

Making an online course is a good home-based business concept because it requires no special equipment and can be done by anybody, even if you're not an expert in video production. After all, the quality of education you offer is really important, and you can still produce excellent material even if you work from home.

You can sell these services through a website or on "gig economy" sites such as Fiverr. YouTube is another great option. Often, people will start a channel showing them enjoying or discussing their hobby and then link recorded lessons in the video description. Websites such as Vimeo are helpful for selling these tutorial videos. You can also sign up for other online platforms which will connect you to students. Just make sure to do your research before making any commitments.

17.
PATREON

Patreon has become a popular crowdfunding website that millions of people use to raise money for their services. Patreon contributors charge their followers monthly to receive various content including art, podcasts, music, and writing, among other things. Although Patreon is most commonly used by artists, a short internet search will reveal all kinds of products and services offered. The big thing to remember is that your fans are paying to support you. They want to see the behind-the-scenes magic and access content not found on your other platforms.

Running a successful Patreon account is a great way for you to make money as a side hustle, you just need to figure out what to offer your followers. Will you be creating some original art for them? Will you be writing something that only your Patreon subscribers can read? What can you create that people would be willing to pay for? Blooper reels, longer uncut videos, informal discussions between friends, personal videos revealing more about your inspiration and life, how-to videos, quizzes, etc. These are all solid ideas for additional content. Just keep in mind that these people are paying to support you in hopes of seeing more of you than the one-dimensional sliver displayed to the public.

Once you have an idea, setting up a Patreon account is quick and easy. The hardest part of this gig is finding people to pay for your content. Many people will use their social media and YouTube accounts to draw people to their Patreon accounts. Many writers and artists will use video content as "teaser" material to advertise for their Patreon. For example, if you knit or refurbish furniture, you might create a YouTube video showing off the finished project or a condensed version of the creation process. At the end of the video, you can encourage viewers to visit your Patreon account where you show them the entire step-by-step process for creating their own similar project.

The nice thing about this is that you can accomplish three side gigs at once. If you record yourself as you create goods, you can put an edited "highlight" reel on YouTube, which could possibly make money later down the road if you are ever monetized. Then give the full video showing how you made your creation to your Patreon subscribers, and finally, sell the created product on any of the platforms we've mentioned earlier in this book.

You'll also need to ensure that whatever you produce for your followers, you produce it often. People will not be willing to pay monthly for a Patreon account that hardly ever delivers. Remember that if you are asking for money, you need to be sure that you're giving a consistent stream of unique content to the people who are supporting you.

18.
BECOME AN INSTAGRAM INFLUENCER

Around the world, one billion users visit Instagram each month. Upwards of 500 million users connect to the network each day from across the world. Being an Instagram influencer has become as much a hobby as it is a side gig. Many users have attempted to gain the influencer title for status purposes even more than for monetary reasons.

Because of its current popularity, there is a lot of competition, and the concept itself is slightly vague and muddled from overuse. So, what is an Instagram influencer exactly? The term can apply to anyone whose account is popular enough to influence trends and the decisions of others. This gig doesn't pay directly, but it has the potential to make a good deal of money if used properly.

There are many companies and businesses that will pay to be featured on popular Instagram accounts. The biggest thing is to create a niche. For example, theming your posts toward health, fitness, and wellness, will create affiliate marketing and sponsorship opportunities from various businesses in these markets. In addition, if you are an influencer who generates inspiring content, it will be easier to affiliate market and sell ad space once you already have a following.

There are some things you should keep in mind!

- There are many scam artists online claiming to offer ambassador programs. You can tell these apart from legitimate offers because they will offer free, cheap products and then charge overly expensive shipping rates for their "free" goods.
- It is ideal to plan your content in advance. The goal here is to create an aesthetic that is visually pleasing.

- Post consistently and use the tools on your account to track the best times to post that will give you the highest engagement rates.
- Keep track of your engagement rates and use those numbers when applying for affiliate marketing opportunities.
- Engage authentically with your followers' content.
- Keep to a small niche that is close to your heart.

Use your hashtag realty wisely by keeping up on which tags are trending and the current standards for posting them. For example, at one point in time using the full thirty hashtags available was recommended. Then over time that method became unpopular as it appeared "desperate" to "Zoomers." By tracking trends, you can discover the best way to use hashtags, and you do want to use them!

Another tip for hashtags is to place them in the comment section rather than in your caption to avoid a cluttered appearance. In the comments section if you place five sets of ellipses on five separate line breaks before your hashtags, it will automatically collapse the list, so that people will only see (…) instead of all your hashtags.

Building a presence on this platform also makes it easier to excel at the other side gigs listed in this book.

19.
RUN FACEBOOK AND INSTAGRAM ADS FOR SMALL BUSINESSES

This is another side gig that overlaps the skills from other sections in this book. With the rise in social media's presence in our society, there are increasing opportunities for people to make money off popular accounts. One of these ways is through publishing ads for small companies.

There is no experience needed for this gig. Both Facebook and Instagram have made it easy to run ads and control the amount of money you spend daily and weekly on running these ads. There are tons of small businesses with marketing funds looking for more people to push their products for them.

There are many companies with the funds to pay influencers a couple of thousand dollars a month to manage their Facebook ads. That could be you! It really isn't that hard to turn this into a side hustle that pays well. All you need to know is how to look for them and which niches to target.

Simply said, running Facebook ad campaigns for customers is all about Facebook ad management.

The ad manager takes the goals of a client into consideration and then develops visuals, text, and target markets in an effort to achieve those goals at the lowest cost possible. They may also write sales text, produce graphics, and manage the advertising budget.

Although both Facebook and Instagram offer tools to help gain the most traffic possible from ads, you should still understand what goes into developing a social media ad side hustle prior to jumping in headlong with managing advertising. You can find courses that will teach you everything you need to know all over the web. They might cost a few bucks, but they are very much worth it if you are planning to take this side gig seriously.

20.
PROOFREAD FOR CONTENT WRITERS AND SMALL BUSINESSES

When you see an ad, press release, or any sort of written content — whether it's on Facebook, in the newspaper, or on a billboard — you are seeing content that has moved through a long list of people who have had a hand in making it 100% ready for public consumption.

A major part of that process is proofreading. For years now, proofreaders have been the unsung heroes of nearly every industry. Their meticulous work is what keeps grammatical errors at bay in a ton of different fields. Now, it is important to remember that not everyone can be a proofreader. This is one of those jobs that requires a lot of practice and knowledge to execute well.

Although you do not need a degree from a university, it is highly recommended to take courses, study, and practice before applying for any proofreading jobs. There are a ton of manuals and workbooks that can help you hone your craft. Once you've practiced, and then practiced some more, it is recommended to take on pro bono or low-paying gigs at first to build experience and a reputation.

A good place to find entry-level jobs is on freelance websites. It is extremely important that you are honest about your experience and do not oversell your abilities. There are many rules to the English language that are not taught in high school or the early years of college. Although this is a skill that is honed through practice, you should be realistic and forthright about your abilities. After all, it's not just your reputation on the line, but the reputation of everyone involved.

21.
TAKE ONLINE SURVEYS

You might have seen ads online telling you that you can make money by simply answering questions. Just spend twenty minutes filling out this survey and the money is yours, they say. Get paid for your opinions, they say. It's all so easy, they promise.

No way that's true, right? Wrong. There are a lot of survey sites online that are truly looking for people to answer questions, give feedback, and help companies get a good handle on what the general public thinks about their ideas or products. If you are looking to start a side hustle that pays for your opinions, you can make that happen. Keep in mind that while it is easy to fill out surveys, they are time-consuming, and the pay varies dramatically depending on who is sponsoring the questionnaire.

But what are these surveys about? Well, honestly, they concern a lot of things related to commerce. Often they will ask questions like:

- Would you buy a product named _____?
- How do you feel about this advertisement?
- How often do you use a product like this?

These are just examples, but almost all survey questions online are about helping companies create products that will fly off the shelves and figuring out who will purchase them when they do.

There are many sites out there attempting to woo you to take their surveys. There are a few extremely important things before you start filling out questionnaires. Although you'll be given several questions related to occupation, age, ethnicity, location, languages spoken, and more when you complete the survey forms, there are many questions these surveys should **not** ask you. It is extremely important you never give anyone your:

- Phone number
- Physical address
- Credit card information

Any websites requesting this type of information are most likely trying to scam you and sell your information to other companies. If you input any of this data you could face everything from spam calls to identity theft! So, please be careful.

In addition, it is highly recommended that you set up a separate e-mail account before getting started with taking surveys. This is simply because these websites will often send you many, many messages updating you whenever there is a new survey you are qualified to take. I promise you, you'll be quite happy to have a separate e-mail account to handle the influx of messages.

Now, we've discussed the risks and nuances of this side hustle—it's time to get into the good stuff! There are many reputable websites that you can sign up with. They will ask you a variety of questions that are used to connect you with the most relevant surveys.

Why? It's because survey firms are interested in the responses from demographic groups. Maybe they'll only want males of a particular age who attended college but never graduated, or something precise like that. Other times they'll only want young folks between the ages of 25 and 34 who travel frequently. The greatest strategy is to just be honest when filling out your information as you sign up.

There is usually at least one terrible survey site for every excellent one. Below is a list of reputable survey websites.

- Branded Surveys
- Inbox Dollars
- Survey Junkie
- Swag Bucks
- Toluna
- I-Say (IPSOS)
- LifePoints
- Pinecone Research
- YouGov

- Marketagent
- Valued Opinions

Although most of these websites are geared toward surveys for product and consumer research, some of them will ask your opinion on social issues, and others will pay handsomely for actual product testing. There are also movies and games available for review. This is a great side hustle to complete during idle time such as watching TV or waiting at the doctor's office.

22.
PINTEREST VIRTUAL ASSISTANT

If you have used Pinterest, you have seen how many companies are using it as a way to drum up business and draw in new customers. However, many of these companies don't run their Pinterest accounts themselves. In fact, it is rare that companies and businesses have the time to run these marketing campaigns and many of them rely on Pinterest virtual assistants to get this job done.

A Pinterest virtual assistant is responsible for boosting organic traffic to the clients' sales pages and websites. Even if you're just starting out, you can still charge $25–$30 per hour for this side hustle. With additional expertise, you could charge up to $100 per hour! And that's especially true if you already use Pinterest enough to understand how the social network operates and are up to date on the most current trends.

The next question is, where do you find these clients? The best place to start, especially as you gain experience, is with any friend or family member who has their own business. Offer low rates or pro bono work until you get a handle on the job.

From there, you can advertise on social media, a website, or put out job postings and create packages on freelance websites such as Fiverr. The undeniable truth is that many small companies are realizing how important social media marketing is. Additionally, almost no organization can afford to do this themselves. These businesses need creative and social people to build their aesthetic, create themed boards, answer messages, engage with potential clients, run and manage ads, etc. All of these tasks are time-consuming for a business owner but can be seen as a fun opportunity to make some extra cash for the right person!

23.
SELL PRINTABLES
ON ETSY

Etsy has become one of the most popular sites on the web for people to buy and sell hand-crafted items. From artwork to books to clothing, jewelry, and more—Etsy has it all. However, you don't need to be a skilled craftsman to turn a profit. In fact, with some practice, you can create a nice side hustle by selling printables!

We've already covered drop-shipping, coffee mugs, and t-shirts, but this section is dedicated to creations that customers can print straight from their computer. Printables are fantastic because the majority of them can be created within a few hours. You make them one time, and then people can purchase them over and over again. All you have to do is pull the document from its saved computer folder and send it on over to the customer once they purchase it.

Although these do require a bit of creativity, most of them can be created with basic computer skills. Here are a few ideas to get you started:

- Calendars
- Checklists (Chores, Hygiene Routines, Self-Care, etc.)
- Meal and Shopping Planning

- Templates (Think paper dolls and snowflakes)
- Coloring Pages
- Recipes
- Blank Recipe Pages
- Mazes, Scavenger Hunts, and Word Puzzles
- Planners (Holidays, Weddings, Events, etc.)
- Habit Trackers

To get started with this side hustle, set up a shop on Etsy. Be careful to fill out all of the prompted fields. Create your printables. You can find inspiration by looking at other products, on websites such as Pinterest, and through general search engines. Most of these can be created by utilizing pre-made text boxes and borders combined with breaking goals and projects down into smaller steps for people to fill out.

Once you have your products, list them on Etsy and sell them. When people purchase the product, simply send them a PDF version (this is not necessary but looks more professional) of the product. These same printables can also be listed on websites such as Fiverr.

24.
REFURBISH FURNITURE

Everyone has that old sofa or dresser that is a little past its prime. Most of the time, people will just throw these items out. You have seen them near dumpsters, waiting to be picked up by the trash collectors and thrown away forever.

But it doesn't have to be that way. In fact, there is a way that you can make some serious cash with reclaimed furniture. And the best news of all is that you don't even have to be a master at any skills to get started.

There are dozens of videos and tutorials online that will teach you how to take rough-looking furniture and turn it into something that looks and feels brand new. It's a good idea to peruse some of these resources for inspiration and an idea of what tools you might need. Some of the most common items are paint, sandpaper, hammer, nails, screws, screwdriver, fabric, and glue. Although the materials you use will vary greatly depending on the furniture you are refurbishing and what you are wanting to do to improve it.

There are a few options for places to find furniture. Although you may be able to find pieces discarded near local dumpsters, you'll have more luck scanning Craigslist and Facebook Marketplace for cheap and free items. There are many people who are hoping to unload old furniture for just about nothing. Try to find what is cheapest and start from there. You will have to go pick up the furniture but once you pay for it, it's yours to play around with. Some fun starter ideas might include:

- Use hemp rope and glue to transform old tires into creative patio furniture.
- Transform broken-down dressers and desks into unique plant boxes for gardens.
- Reupholster furniture (there are detailed tutorials on how to replace the padding and fabrics).
- Sandpaper, a fresh stain, and screws can fix up most worn-down wooden furniture.

After it's done and it looks the way you want, you should then hop back online, to Facebook Marketplace, eBay, or any number of other sites that sell hand-crafted items. Make sure that you take terrific photos of your work so you can really show off how it looks.

25.
WALK DOGS/PET SIT

Are you an animal lover? Do you enjoy hanging out with cats or dogs? Do you love getting outside and taking long walks, being in touch with nature, and getting fresh air while getting paid for it?

If you answered yes to those questions then you are in luck because there are quite a few side hustle options for someone who enjoys playing with animals.

There are numerous people who own a dog but don't have a schedule that allows them to walk their pet as often as they need. Many people work and are away from home for most of the day. That means their dogs are stuck inside, itching to either get out of the house or the backyard. This is when pet sitting comes in handy.

But how do you get started being a professional dog walker? You can start with fliers and post them throughout your neighborhood. Most post offices and small grocery stores still have a public bulletin board as well. These are sure to attract a few eyes from people who live near you.

Another great approach is to create ads or posts on Facebook, Instagram, and other social media sites. Make sure to underline the fact that you love animals (if you have any of your own, perhaps you should post pictures or describe them) and that you will treat any and all animals with respect and care. The last thing anyone wants is to be unsure of the person watching their pets.

It is vital you always remember that people love their pets as if they are members of their family. So, you need to go above and beyond to convey the fact that any animal in your care will not only be safe but loved and cared for too.

Your customers are putting a very precious life in your hands when they allow you to interact with their pets, even if it's just for a short amount of time.

In addition to fliers, there are a number of apps available such as NextDoor and Rover that you can use to reach out to people. NextDoor is particularly great because it allows you to alert people who live near you. It is recommended to start with a small circle of people using your services before you expand and try to find more clients.

26.
RENT OUT
YOUR CAR

Like many things these days, you can now use apps to rent out your car to tourists for long-term excursions or to your neighbors for an hour or two of errands.

How does sharing your automobile as a side hustle work? Well, exactly like you'd imagine. You share your car, and you get paid. The majority of car-sharing apps merely demand a brief form and an examination before you can begin earning money. This can take as little as a day to set up!

The procedure for renting out your automobile is quite easy after registration. You specify the hours and locations when your automobile will be available for use. Other people reserve the car through the app and after reviewing the request, you can accept or reject it.

Most car-sharing applications demand up-front payments, so you have the money prior to the car ever leaving your place. You don't have to fear someone mistreating your ride because there are severe penalties for abuse and late pickups. After clearing out trash and personal items, deliver the car to the pickup site. You can either hand the keys over face-to-face or store them in a secure location for pickup. After they deposit the keys in a secure location, you go get your car and drive it home. It is important to pay for good insurance that covers basic vehicle repairs.

That's how simple it is. But which car-sharing app is best? According to Hyrecar, you could earn an additional $12,000 each year! With a vast network of 1,500 towns around the country, their competitor Turo touts an annual revenue of more than $10,500 for your ride and also doesn't require any prior car-sharing expertise to join. Getaround is unique in that if you're a part of a bigger organization, they may host your whole company fleet in addition to working with individual car owners.

As you can see, there are a few growing options for you to choose from if you wish to rent out your car. It's all fairly easy and straightforward. If you have the car, you have the ability to make money. It requires time to upkeep your car, maintain its cleanliness, and keep it in working order but the payout you'll receive will make it worth it.

27.
HOUSE-SIT

House-sitting is a great method to make a side income, especially if doing house chores does not phase you. Many homeowners engage house sitters to take care of their dogs, collect mail and newspapers, adjust alarms, and tend to their plants. Some homeowners also want their property to appear inhabited to deter burglars. Keeping the lights on or having activity in the house when someone is away is a wonderful way to prevent crime. Having said that, some clients might request that you only visit the residence once or twice each day rather than staying there full-time.

There is always a need for house sitters, especially among pet-owners' homes. Kennels are often costly and uncomfortable for the animals. Providing house-sitting services is a logical additional side hustle for someone who's already into pet-sitting. People will pay handsomely to ensure the security of their home, belongings, and loved ones.

You can find potential house-sitting jobs through the various channels we've mentioned in previous sections, such as the NextDoor app. There are also companies that specialize in connecting house sitters to clients. However, working through these companies will require more work because they are careful to vet each potential house sitter.

The amount you are paid will vary depending on where you are house-sitting. Obviously, the more space you need to look over, and the more tasks you need to do, the more you'll get paid. The compensation is established depending on the quantity of duties allocated and the location. In general, if you are asked to temporarily live in the house or have to take care of pets, you may charge extra.

There are some disadvantages to keep in mind before committing to being a house sitter. Here are a few:

- House-sitting is not a side hustle that will pay all of the bills.
- Homeowners can be rather critical and particular about the care their house and pets receive.
- Chores and cleaning are expected, and there is a high level of responsibility associated with this job.
- It is always possible that the animals may not like you, which could be difficult at best.

Despite these drawbacks, this can be a fun way to earn a little extra cash each month.

28.
GET CASH BACK
WHILE SHOPPING

You probably already shop a lot in your regular day-to-day life. Whenever you fill up your home with groceries, you are actually doing something that you could soon be getting paid for. Yes, it's true, there are apps that actually send money back to you when you make purchases.

You have the chance to earn cash back on eligible purchases made through cash-back apps and websites. These apps are becoming more popular as legions of people find out about them and want to use them, so if you are hoping to turn cash-back apps into your full-time side hustle, you'll want to get right to it.

How do they work? You can use cash-back apps to find various specials, browse deals, and identify available goods to make qualifying transactions. The cash-back app receives a fee from retailers for directing users to their websites. Upon receiving a photo of your receipt, the app will split the commission with you. It truly is that easy.

One of the top cash-back applications for online purchasing is Rakuten. Simply sign up for a free account, choose the online retailer, and then go to shop as usual to get started.

You'll then notice cash refunded to the account in approximately two days.

When you purchase online with Swagbucks, you can get cash back and make savings with promo codes. This is a well-known rewards website where you can obtain gift cards for online activities. In other words, you'll be paid to do surveys, make purchases online, view movies, play games, and more.

With the free Ibotta app, you can get cash back on regular purchases like food, clothing, transportation, and shopping. You only need to sign up for a free account, locate and add incentives offered by your preferred stores, and then begin earning cash back as quickly as your transaction is processed. This is one of the top grocery-related cash-back applications.

The truth is that there are plenty of cash-back apps that are growing in popularity these days. You will have your choice to pick from. You could use multiple apps or just focus on a single one you like best. No matter your approach, make sure you use it often, as that will be the only way you'll actually start making a solid amount of money. You'll need to use the apps often, shop a lot, and really expect a slow drip of money coming into your account. You won't become rich overnight when you use cashback apps as a side hustle, but you will make some good money over time!

29.
SHOPIFY

Physical stores are becoming increasingly competitive online. You cannot shop at a place that doesn't have an online presence now. There are so many options. Seemingly every single business has an online component to it.

You may have considered running a traditional brick-and-mortar store as a possible career choice. However, today there are other options that require lower start-up costs and fewer long-term commitments. One of these options is the online store platform Shopify.

Shopify aims to help make running a business, selling products, and creating a loyal legion of customers much easier. With Shopify, customers can conveniently make purchases online and have access to the finest prices on a worldwide scale. It's fantastic because it's ideal for vendors who are first opening an internet business.

Getting started with Shopify is rather straightforward. Simply:

- Sign up
- Spend some time filling out all fields

- Post a product (you can use ideas from other sections in this book to create your products through print-on-demand, printables, or drop-shipping options)
- Customize the look of your store
- Set up payment following the site's detailed instructions

Although Shopify makes it easy to get started, it is good to keep in mind that Shopify will charge fees based on the plan you choose.

30.
PLAY GAMES
FOR CASH

Although some of the websites listed in the survey section will pay people to give their opinions on games, there are some games that will pay you to play them consistently. Often these games will pay out whenever you win. The cash-outs will vary. You will not win cash every time you play, but if you're going to play phone games anyway, this is a good way to drum up more cash.

How do these games afford to pay you to play, you ask? Well, this is actually the most important part of this section! These games will often sell the data they collected from you to other companies—information such as:

- Web and search history
- Locations
- Purchases
- Apps
- Contacts

This sounds scary; however, many apps that you are already using are doing the same thing. Every social media app employs similar tactics, and there are ways to protect yourself if you decide to play these games for cash.

Another way these apps make money is by running ads. Companies will pay the game for ad space in an attempt to generate sales from players. Some games may also offer in-app purchases to earn extra money from players. Always use safe payment services such as PayPal or Amazon gift cards. Never put your bank account information directly into these games. One last thing—check the cash-out requirements before playing. Some of these games will pay you, but the requirements to actually cash out are near impossible to meet. If you keep these things in mind, you can play and earn cash safely!

Here are some of the top games that pay either in cash or gift cards:

- Lucktastic
- Bingo Clash
- Solitaire Cash

- Brain Battle
- Givling
- QuickRewards Network
- Bananatic

This is not a get rich quick scheme. However, if you are going to play phone games anyway, you should do it in a way that can earn you rewards and money.

31.
COMPLETE TASKS ON TASKRABBIT

You might not have heard of TaskRabbit but it's a great side gig that millions of people are using these days. It's yet another job, like Uber or Lyft or DoorDash, that you can pick up and put down whenever you want. You make your own schedule, work at your own pace, and follow the beat of your own drum. Really, isn't that what the life of a side hustler is all about?

Simply put, TaskRabbit is a program that puts people who need tasks done alongside people who can do said tasks. If you like the thought of finishing random odd jobs for other people as a side gig then TaskRabbit could be perfect for you. You might be putting together furniture, helping someone move, cleaning up for a big party, or dropping off items that someone needs delivered. You really don't know what tasks you might get with TaskRabbit and that's one of the job's more interesting aspects.

Once you download the TaskRabbit app, you can quickly follow the process of becoming a "Tasker", one of the people running around town doing odd jobs. The app will send you notifications when there are available jobs in your area, and you can then confirm or deny that you want to do them.

One of the stand-out things about TaskRabbit is that you set your own rate. That means that you get to decide how much you are getting paid. This allows you to make a lot more money if you go about things in the right way.

If you stay competitive and charge a rate that someone can't say no to, you are likely to land more jobs more frequently. And there are some jobs that are harder than others. If you are willing to take on these jobs — usually physical — then you can make a prettier penny because you are tackling the tasks that other people don't want to. As you can see, TaskRabbit is the sort of side hustle that will reward you based upon how hard you are willing to work and how much effort and energy you're willing to put in.

You can finish these odd jobs whenever you like. But you need to make sure you have a few things in order before signing up for TaskRabbit. You will need:

- A valid social security card

- To be 18 years or older
- To live in a city that supports TaskRabbit
- An active checking account
- To own a smartphone
- To complete a background check

Sure, that's a lot of things to check off the list. But once you do, you'll soon be working odd jobs all over town and making serious bank.

You have probably finished a few odd jobs in your life, especially if you have friends who have asked you to help them move or set up furniture. Why not get paid to do so with TaskRabbit?

32.
TEACH ART LESSONS

Are you an artistic person? Do you have a hobby that you can share with others? Whether you enjoy painting, drawing, whittling, or knitting, you can make money by teaching others what you know.

When it comes to selling art classes, you don't need to be an expert or hold a degree, but you do need to have more experience than your audience. For example, if you only know how to knit a simple scarf, you probably wouldn't want to attempt to create lessons targeting knitters who have mastered intricate sweater patterns. This side hustle is one that requires passion and a knack for breaking down skills into bite-sized lessons.

Once you've decided what kind of art you will teach, there are a plethora of platforms designed for selling courses. In previous sections, we've already mentioned Patreon, but here are some others to check out:

- Udemy
- The Abundant Artist
- Skill Share
- Vimeo

At the risk of redundancy, it is best to overlap the ideas from multiple sections of this book to work together to make even more money. When creating these courses, you can advertise by creating "teaser" content featuring finished projects or small sections of video on social media and then providing links to the full courses.

Another option is to teach in-person courses. These are a little more time-consuming but can be quite worth it. More and more people are enjoying adult art classes where they can walk out with a painting they've created. To get (or create) one of these jobs, you need to be able to teach anyone to paint interesting images by breaking it down into simple shapes. There are plenty of ideas online using search terms such as "paint night" or "paint and drink." These paintings are often simple landscapes that can be broken down into basic shapes. You can set up these nights by contacting local bars in your area or presenting your paint night idea to nearby art studios. It is important to keep in mind that licensing is required for painting nights that involve alcohol, which is why it is recommended to collaborate with venues that already hold the proper documentation.

Another option is to advertise on the good old bulletin boards and online equivalents for prospective students in your area. These can be found:

- At small grocery stores
- The post office
- NextDoor app
- Craigslist
- Facebook

Regardless of what you wish to teach, the most important aspect of selling these courses is passion! Show the world what you can do and why you love it and make money in the process!

33.
RENT OUT
YOUR POOL

Everyone loves swimming in the pool during the summer. There is nothing like splashing around, swimming with friends, and having a wet and wild time when the weather is hot. Often, once people purchase a personal pool they find they don't occupy it as much as they thought they would.

Thanks to modern technology, there is an app called Swimply, which allows you to rent out your pool to strangers for a few hours at a time.

Swimply is similar to an Airbnb for swimming pools, offering a searchable database of approved local private pools that can be rented out by the hour without requiring overnight accommodations.

Owners of private home pools can interact with others who want to utilize one through an online pool-sharing website. A pool can be rented out for a few hours or a whole day by those who don't own one, while pool owners are paid for their unused facilities.

Many individuals are utilizing the platform to identify nearby pools, as seen by the more than 75,000 reservations made in the year 2021 alone. Similar to a housing platform, users can scroll through listings, see images, and read reviews.

When considering this as a side gig, it is important to keep in mind that not all pools are approved for use by Swimply. You need to make sure your pool is clean, and the area around it is safe. You also need to ensure easy access to the backyard (or wherever you've planted your pool), so people won't need to invade your private space.

Swimply is a great way to let other people use what you already have: a backyard pool. However, there will be a lot of hoops to jump through to become approved, and it could create a few other hassles too. Your yard might become something of a mess after a big party thrown by strangers. Also, you'll need to put extra work and attention into making sure your pool is in good working order. The last thing you want is a pool that looks awful and beat up. There are drawbacks, but more and more people are signing up to make a little extra cash on the side using Swimply.

34.
BECOME A
BOOKKEEPER

Bookkeeping is needed in every business, economy, and country on this planet. Despite the fact that it doesn't get the recognition it merits, everyone needs bookkeeping.

An accounting side hustle is a fantastic method to make money if you are confident with numbers and have outstanding organizational abilities. To begin, you don't even need to hold a valid CPA license. If starting a bookkeeping business appeals to you, the following guide might be helpful.

Prior to starting anything, pick a single area of bookkeeping to concentrate on. This will enable you to create a unique identity and draw in a specific type of consumer. For instance, you may be an expert in tax preparation or payroll auditing. Additionally, you can narrow your emphasis even more by specializing in handling the books for particular kinds of firms. Prior bookkeeping expertise is a bonus, but it's not required. Just make sure to have a well-thought-out game plan before starting your business.

Although becoming a CPA is not needed to begin a bookkeeping gig, you need at the very least to be familiar with the fundamentals of accounting, and the more experience you have, the better. There are a few terms you should be comfortable with, including:

- Accounts Payable
- Accounts Receivable
- Assets
- Balance Sheet
- Capital
- Cost of Goods Sold
- Depreciation
- Equity
- Expenses
- General Ledger
- Income Statements
- Journals
- Liabilities
- Payroll
- Revenue
- Trial Balance

It is also recommended to familiarize yourself with Quickbooks and tax law and complete at least some training before offering your services. Most small businesses are extremely frustrated with trying to sort out their books on their own. This is where even entry-level bookkeepers can come in and save the day! The most important thing to remember, as with all of these side hustles, is to be honest and transparent about your experience level so that your customers fully understand what they are paying for.

35.
CLEAN HOUSES

Here is yet another great way to make some extra money and, again, it's something that you have done all your life: cleaning house.

To clean other people's houses, you should post your services on a social media site or a website like Craigslist, Care.com, or NextDoor. Other options include making fliers to post in your area and offering discounts to people who refer new clients to you. Word of mouth is often one of the best ways to market services of this nature. Make sure you have some photos showing your previous work and what you can do. Show off your skills! This is the best way to convince people that you can clean their homes.

There are some things to keep in mind. For example, most cleaning services are requested to work all kinds of hours to fit around their client's schedule. You'll also need to supply your own cleaning supplies and be able to transport them between job sites. In addition, this job will require licensing, depending on how much money you make. The amount you can make before jumping through these hoops will depend on where you live; most information can be accessed easily online.

36.
BECOME A
SOCIAL MEDIA
MANAGER

Many businesses have Facebook, Instagram, and Twitter pages but need someone to run them. That's where you and your new side hustle can come in handy!

Being a social media manager means that you will be running a social media page—or pages—for a business. This involves a few things. Firstly, you need to understand the business your clients are running, the industry,, and the customers they have. You can find this by conducting research online. Study other successful accounts in the same niche and industry to gain insight on how to promote the brand.

This side hustle is perfect for the person who has already learned about the most common platforms through personal experience and regular use. Many businesses know they need to post daily to build an organic following, but they do not have the time to keep up with their social media presence while they are running their business. As a social media manager, you will create meaningful posts, generate discussions, and manage message responses and frequently asked questions, among other tasks that the business may require.

An easy way to get started with this job is to offer a low-priced package on freelance websites such as Fiverr or ask local businesses if you can help them. There are many articles, videos, and online courses available for free that can improve your skills. With enough experience, this side hustle can be quite lucrative.

37.
SELL SERVICES
ON FIVERR

We've mentioned it a lot in this book already, but have you heard of Fiverr? If not, it's definitely a site that you should keep near and dear to you if you are looking for side hustles.

Fiverr is a site that helps you find people who are willing to pay you for just about anything. There are people with various talents, various rates, and various needs all over the site. I have even seen people sell their "best advice" and pre-made videos with romance tips.

On the website, you will offer three package rates: Basic, Standard, and Premium. These packages can range from $5 up to hundreds of dollars. For example, let's say you offered to write articles for people's blogs. A basic package may include one 1000-word article with one revision, a standard package may include one 1500-word article with two revisions, and the premium package may include two articles with unlimited revisions. These are random examples, of course, but essentially you want to offer three pricing tiers to customers.

Fiverr can be difficult because it is often hard to break through the crowd of all the other people trying to land jobs. The best way to handle this is to start your pricing low and build up a reputation through customer reviews. As you provide consistent, high-quality work to clients, they will leave you five-star reviews and comments, which will draw in more customers. Once you start building a solid foundation, you can increase your prices to reflect your skillset.

38.
FLIP CARS

What is flipping cars, and how do you do it?

It's pretty much what you'd imagine: you take a car that is a little beat up, improve and enhance it, and then you resell it for more than you bought it for. Simple, right? Well, yes and no. If you know a lot about cars, then this entire process *is* simple. This is most definitely an ideal side hustle for the mechanically inclined.

Often, people will sell their cars at lower rates than they're worth simply because they do not know what is wrong with them or they've recently upgraded to a better vehicle. People with some automotive know-how can look for deals by comparing the listed prices to the *Kelley Blue Book* prices. Sometimes people are able to spin a profit with as little as detailing the vehicle and topping off the oil; other times, the car might require parts to be replaced or dents repaired.

When you're about to purchase a potential vehicle to flip, it is important to know what is wrong with it before buying. You can do this by investing in a computer reader, which will produce a code when hooked up to the vehicle. From there, you can look up the code on your phone and see the estimated cost for parts.

If you are interested in this but you don't have the necessary skills, you can still pursue this option by building a network. Talk to your motorhead friends or go to local auto shops and find out which ones will work for just the labor costs and let you buy parts from the cheapest places. The biggest thing to remember is that you want to turn a profit, so make sure to include the costs of time, parts, labor, and the initial purchase into the amount you are reselling it for.

39.
SELL LESSON PLANS, CHEAT SHEETS, AND ACTIVITY SHEETS

This side hustle is ideal for teachers and childcare providers. However, it is not limited to educational professionals. Teachers—whether in a classic academic institution or the comforts of home—use lesson plans to guide their way through teaching students various topics.

If you think back to your school days or pull out a textbook, you'll most likely notice a pattern. Most lessons include learning objectives, a lecture or main lesson, and then discussion questions or an activity. A teacher's lesson plan will usually include more material to help with teaching, including:

- Pre-requisites
- Materials needed
- Lesson procedure
- A reflection
- A way to assess the student's retention

Here's the thing, teachers **need** lesson plans every single day. Hours upon hours go into creating these, only to be used once a year. In addition, parents who are homeschooling might struggle to come up with good material to help their children learn. This is where you can help. You can create these lessons and then sell them to multiple teachers — earning you money and saving them time (and frustration)!

There are many resources online that will guide you through getting started. Websites like "Teachers Pay Teachers" are good places to start. In addition to lesson plans, there is also a demand for:

- Worksheets (everything from learning how to write to basic math)
- Cheat sheets (quick lists of important dates, figures, measurements, etc.)
- Exams and quizzes (testing knowledge of common subjects)

With a little creativity, research, and time, you can save teachers everywhere a massive hassle by creating these for them.

40.
START A
YOUTUBE CHANNEL

This is another side hustle we've referenced repeatedly throughout this book. Now, it is important to keep in mind that it takes time to make money from a YouTube channel; however, it can also be used to help support your other side hustles. You can create a YouTube account based on any kind of subject matter. It is recommended, though, that you keep monetization in mind from the very start.

Although the regulations change from time to time, to be monetized YouTube usually requires:

- 4,000 watch-hours within the previous year
- 1,000 subscribers to your account

There are other requirements, but these are the two basics. I know it seems like a tall order to fill—right now. However, it is not impossible, and it is important to start your YouTube channel as if you know beyond a doubt that you'll be monetized later. One way you can do this is by creating longer videos to make sure that they will be broken up by ads after monetization.

Like most online media, it is recommended to create your channel targeting a specific niche and to post consistently. For example, I personally watch many videos from indie authors about how to write. These YouTubers have a specific theme and aesthetic to their videos.

Other ways you can make money from YouTube include:

- Advertising your products and services
- Partnering with other channels

- Selling other people's products
- Affiliate marketing
- Crowdfunding

This is not a get-rich-quick option; however, it is a fantastic tool to support your other side hustles. As mentioned in previous sections, many creators will use their YouTube channels as "teasers" for paid lessons and content on other marketplaces. For example, those indie writers I mentioned earlier often link their Patreon, books, and podcast links in the description of their short "How-To" videos.

If you don't know what to create or maybe just have no interest in a personal account, you can always offer to create content for other small businesses. Time is money, and many small businesses have the money but not the time.

41.
MOBILE AUTO DETAILING BUSINESS

Here is a concept that wasn't even thought about just ten years ago, but now is a great way for you to make a lot of money! A mobile auto detailing business travels to the car to get the work done instead of having a stationary shop.

Car detailers clean and restore a car's condition to as close to new as possible. This job is ideal for people who enjoy cleaning and have a high attention to detail. There are plenty of free videos online to help learn the trade. From there, when you feel like you have enough talent to start a business, you absolutely *need* a social media presence. This is the best way for you to start to find customers.

Are there car enthusiast Facebook groups in your area? If so, make sure you subscribe to them and stay connected to them and the people involved. This is a great way to meet like-minded car lovers who would make for terrific clients in this new field you're diving into.

42.
INVEST IN
REAL ESTATE

Real estate investment is a side hustle idea that may be both rewarding and profitable. Prospective homeowners can utilize leverage to purchase a property, more so than stock investing, by paying a percentage of the entire cost up front and then working off the remainder, plus the interest, over time.

Even while a regular mortgage typically demands a 30% down payment, in some circumstances a mere 5% down payment is sufficient to buy the entire home. Both real estate flippers and landlords are empowered by the ability to assume possession of the asset as soon as the paperwork is signed and can acquire another mortgage on their homes to pay down payments on more properties.

Real estate investors may develop a comprehensive investment program by paying a very modest portion of a property's overall worth upfront, whether they use their assets to create rental income or to pass the time until the ideal selling opportunity presents itself. Real estate offers potential for profit regardless of how the market is performing overall, as with any investment.

Obviously, investing in real estate is the sort of side hustle that will take a lot of time, energy, knowledge and, eventually, expertise. So, you need to get started as soon as possible if this is something you want to do. You are never too young to start learning about your local real estate market and teaching yourself what you need to know to become an expert and make this side hustle dream a reality.

43.
CHILDCARE SERVICES

Offering childcare services is the perfect side hustle for parents already staying at home with their children. After all, why not provide additional daycare services to other families in your neighborhood while you're at home taking care of your kids? Due to the high demand for childcare, you may accomplish two goals at once by working as a childcare provider and seeing your own kids more often.

When you want to start a childcare service side hustle, you need a couple of things: people who trust you, a proven track record, and a lot of patience. Parents will not allow you to watch their kids unless they trust you so you, should start by looking after the children of people who know you personally. That way you will have the experience to prove to others that you have what it takes and will keep kids safe and happy no matter how long you're watching them!

Once you are comfortable watching more than just your own children, there are ways to expand this side hustle into a full at-home business. The licensing will vary depending on where you live, but the information is easily accessible online. There are many parents desperate for affordable childcare and starting with references from friends and family is an easy way to get traction.

44.
LANDSCAPE

Via the use of new up-and-coming websites like Greenpal, Takl, Thumbtack, TaskEasy, and others, you can now turn landscaping into a side hustle that can pay out very well all year long.

The way these sites work is that you simply create an account and then advertise your services to people in your area. From there, people will start asking you to mow their lawn, throw out green waste, clean up a garden, and so much more.

These landscaping apps allow you to make your own schedule, move at your own speed, take the jobs you want, and make a lot of money at your own pace. It's great for people who haven't had any formal training in landscaping but just have a natural talent for it.

If you want to turn this side hustle into a real, full-time job, you'd be smart to start your own website advertising your services and your business. Social media pages are also a great way to show people what you can accomplish.

45.
START A
PODCAST

Podcasts have changed from a niche form of entertainment into something that is incredibly successful and can make you a ton of money. But before you start your show, you need to know what you're trying to create.

You may have a podcast idea without a clear target audience in mind but building an audience when people don't know what to anticipate is considerably more difficult. A podcast with no apparent topic is also difficult to promote and distribute.

Choosing a niche does not mean you need to select a topic that is highly specific. Your topic might be incredibly limited or quite wide, but the most important thing is that it is a big enough topic to allow for multiple episodes.

Choosing a target demographic is recommended before starting. An easy way to do this and maintain consistency is to imagine a specific person you are talking to who would be interested in what you have to say. This is also an excellent moment to consider your podcast's purpose. Are you making this podcast to share with a select group of friends, or are you aiming for a wider audience?

Would you like to make your listeners laugh, or is the goal of your podcast to impart knowledge? Early consideration of these issues will help prevent you from veering off course later on.

46.
BECOME A
MOBILE NOTARY

A mobile notary is exactly what it sounds like: a notary public who travels around the city. And it's a good living, either as a side hustle or a full-time job.

Most notaries typically charge between $75 and $200 each visit. This may differ based on a number of variables, such as where you live, the level of demand, and the particulars of each appointment. There are established rates that notaries can charge for particular services in several states.

Unlike some of the jobs suggested in this book, becoming a notary does take a little work in advance. Each U.S. state will have different requirements, which are easily accessed online. Usually this consists of some coursework, an exam, and processing fees. Fingerprinting, a background check, a commission certificate, and a surety bond are also needed. Although the total cost will depend on where you live, this is a lucrative side hustle that usually costs less than $100 to get started.

47.
WATCH VIDEOS

Many websites really pay you to see advertisements, previews, and other material such as movies and TV episodes. While it won't make you wealthy, spending your leisure time online, viewing movies, can earn you prepaid cards and additional cash that could help you save.

For example, a rewards website called MyPoints has been operating since 1996. The business has hundreds of five-star reviews and a high rating from the Better Business Bureau. In addition to coupon savings, MyPoints allows you to use your membership to receive points whenever you make purchases, participate in online surveys, play games, and watch movies.

The same firm that owns MyPoints also owns Swagbucks, a well-known rewards program that was established in 2004. The business has thousands of five-star Trustpilot evaluations and a BBB grade of A.

Kashkick collaborates with businesses who are ready to hear from users like you and learn from their experiences, much like other tried-and-true applications on our list. Kashkick is a reputable website that lets you earn rewards in a variety of ways, including watching videos.

Since all of the websites listed here offer free memberships, feel free to check out a lot of them before settling on a couple that you want to continue with for the long term.

You could be earning money instead of idly browsing social media, emails, or zoning out to videos. The greatest benefit of all? You can start making quick money online right now by sitting on your chair with your smartphone.

48.
SEWING

If you have picked up the skill of sewing over the years, then you have a fun and creative way to make some extra money for yourself.

Let's be honest, there are plenty of people who have sewing needs, and you can totally capitalize on that by starting a sewing side hustle. All you need are the right tools (like a sewing machine), a network of people who need your help, and the determination and drive to work hard.

To start, you should post on Facebook that you are willing to do some sewing work for friends. This is a great way to build experience, show off your skills, and prove to people that you know what you're doing and can efficiently and excellently get the work done.

Take plenty of pictures of your final results, create a website, and then show off your projects. This will attract even more customers because they will see just how well you did. It's like a digital calling card!

You should invest in the best sewing machine and materials when you start this side hustle. That's the greatest way to ensure that the work you put out will be worth the money you charge. As always, start with a lower asking rate and then slowly work your way up as you find more and more customers.

49.
REVIEW AND
WRITE RESUMES

Anyone looking to get a new job will need a resume. It's a vital part of the job hunt and, therefore, an opportunity for you to help—for a fee, of course.

The typical resume writer makes $20 per hour, which is unquestionably a nice wage. Once you have developed a solid reputation as a skilled resume writer in the industry, you might charge between $90 and $120 for a particular resume or CV.

If you want to establish your name, starting with cheaper prices could help you get in the door. However, don't underprice yourself! People will pay well to make sure they are putting their best foot forward. This is another service that can be developed on freelance websites.

50.
REFEREE

Typically, refereeing requires relatively little time dedicated to training. It makes use of your expertise and presumable love for sports and converts it into real money. Sounds like a fantastic bargain, no? It's always a wonderful idea to try to turn what you enjoy into a source of income.

Although it isn't always required, having a basic understanding of your sport of choice is a good place to start. There will also be a broad range of requirements, based on the scale of tournament you are officiating. If you're wanting to develop the abilities required to be a higher-level referee, often local sports clubs will offer clinics to teach new recruits. It's not always the simplest job being a referee. Accepting criticism, whether it's justified or not, is a must.

If you can work three to four games on the weekends, your pay could be close to $300. Yes, being a local ref really can pay that well! Refereeing a sport such as soccer will also improve your health and body because of all of the exercise.

So, you get paid to watch a sport you love, get some exercise in, and really do something that pleases you.

51.
CLINICAL RESEARCH TRIALS

Clinical research trials involve research projects that develop medical techniques in a particular field. Anyone can be compensated to test new medications, medical gadgets, treatments, or goods as a clinical trial volunteer. These trials help physicians heal and diagnose patients and prescribe medication more effectively.

They aid with the introduction of novel medical procedures and practices that can enhance people's lives and treat illnesses. Pharmaceutical firms, academic institutions, healthcare facilities, and manufacturers of medical devices are always searching for the most cutting-edge medical advancements.

In order to gather crucial data for the creation and dissemination of new medical advances, these organizations will support compensated clinical studies. These studies might pay a range from $100 to thousands of dollars. Your compensation will depend on the amount of time you spend, how risky the experiment is, and which field of medicine it is in.

Typically, you will receive payment for each time you attend a trial. A decent generalization is that you'll be paid more the longer the trial lasts. Early phase, experimental studies will also result in higher compensation, due to the increased risk.

There will be many more people evaluated and the compensation will be significantly less in trials that are further along and are categorized as phase three.

All participants are welcome in clinical studies, but every trial will have a unique set of conditions. So just because something pays out well doesn't mean you'll meet the specific requirements to be a part of it. You can visit clinictrials.gov to find actively recruiting trials.

52.
ADVERTISE
ON YOUR CAR

There are many businesses that will compensate you to promote them on your vehicle with decals or covers. Auto advertising organizations hire individuals to drive around town promoting their products.

To get approved, you will need to:

- Complete an application form

- Provide proof of your identity
- Provide an active email address
- Provide contact info and a location

The advertising agency will pair you up with businesses that are relevant to the region where you commute regularly and your driving style.

Once you've been given the go-ahead to start driving, the firm will install a vehicle wrap and start paying you monthly via direct transfer. The money you may make from automobile marketing fluctuates based on how long the campaign lasts.

For the length of the promotion, individuals who work this side job typically get a flat salary of $100 per month. The business you advertised for will then take down the advertisement when the campaign is over.

If you own a car, you are probably already driving around a lot so why wouldn't you want to get paid to do so? Once you apply the ad on your car, you'll start raking in the bucks.

53.
SELL OLD
ELECTRONICS

The world we live in now is full of electronic devices that are cutting edge for a moment before becoming obsolete. So why not make money by getting rid of outdated tech? Yes, you can turn tossing out your old electronics into a side hustle that will pay you for the things you no longer use!

One of the quickest and most reliable websites to sell your unwanted gadgets is Decluttr. The many things you can sell on the site include secondhand DVDs, mobile phones, video games, and other technology.

On Declutter, getting paid is simple. You will first receive a quote for your purchases. All you need to do is send your items to their warehouse if you accept the pricing. Orders are examined the same day a shipment is delivered, and payment is then processed quickly after that.

Sure, you may not make a ton of money by selling old electronics, but it can quickly add up if you are consistent about it. Why just let something collect dust and lay around your home if you can make money off of it instead?

54.
PACKAGE
DELIVERY DRIVER

For brand-new and experienced delivery drivers looking for a reliable source of additional income, Amazon provides a delivery service. For people who don't want to devote themselves to the firm full-time, this is a good choice. However, what precisely is Amazon Flex?

To assist in spreading out the workload of their delivery requirements, Amazon recruits members for their logistical staff. Carriers for Amazon Flex distribute items on the company's behalf, and Amazon compensates them well for the distribution blocks they complete. In essence, they are self-employed independent contractors.

Drivers with Amazon Flex have—you guessed it—flexible hours. The platform has a similar structure to most well-known rideshare apps available today. In most cases, you don't have a regular schedule like you would if you worked a normal job. Instead, you choose when you want to work and follow the schedule you create.

Drivers working for Amazon as independent contractors often make between $18 and $25 per hour. However, on a fortunate day when tips start pouring in, that amount may increase to $30 or even $45. Given that a distribution block provides two- to four-hour periods, you may consistently earn a sizable wage.

55.
GRAPHIC DESIGN

Graphic design jobs were once only available for people with a lot of formal training and years of experience. But that is no longer the case! Nowadays, anyone who spends time learning the field and perfecting their craft can start a graphic design side hustle that will do more than just pay a few bills.

Before you can do anything, you need to make sure you really have some graphic design skills under your belt. A good place to start is free videos, but it is highly recommended to take courses before selling your services. This is another job that will require time to build experience and a reputation. You can get started by selling low-cost packages on Fiverr or searching for entry-level positions on freelance websites. Remember to always be honest about your abilities and limitations. These kinds of side hustles are highly profitable depending entirely on your reputation.

56.
SOCIAL MEDIA
AND SEARCH ENGINE
RATER

Someone who manually evaluates the outcomes of online searches and offers comments on the precision and value of the findings is known as a search engine evaluator. Engineers can modify the search engine algorithm to get the greatest results with the aid of this input.

It's a terrific entry-level work-at-home job since just about anybody with an internet connection, a desire to study, and some basic familiarity with search results can get started. You'll need to have a few things, in terms of both information and expertise: high speed internet, linguistic proficiency, familiarity with search engines, and test-taking abilities.

If you think you have the time and energy for a side hustle like this, you'll need to contact companies such as Appen, Lionbridge, Google, and more. Each of these places offer search engine rating jobs that are available all year round. And they pay quite well too. However, keep in mind that this is a pretty non-stop job!

57.
AIRBNB
EXPERIENCE HOST

Activities that visitors can book through Airbnb during their travels are called "Experiences." In each location, these activities are led by local hosts. They go beyond simple classes or guided excursions. Anyone who enjoys being creative is welcome to apply to participate in the program.

The portal caters to several markets. Some tourists use it to network with newcomers, whereas others use experiences to learn about nearby sites. Experiences have the power to draw both single and group reservations.

Experiences may only be offered by hosts who have received Airbnb's approval. In order to provide an experience, hosts must enroll in the program.

At airbnb.com/host/experiences, users can apply to host an Airbnb Experience. After that, Airbnb will get in touch to inform them of the status of their application. Although it is occasionally less, the waiting period is typically around two weeks.

In order to participate in the Experiences program, hosts must pay Airbnb a commission charge equal to 20% of the total cost. This charge is subtracted when Airbnb processes the payment. Although the cost may seem excessive, it enables Airbnb to offer assistance and management tools for hosts.

58.
WEDDING OFFICIANT

Did you know you can make some seriously good money by marrying two people? It's true, there is a lot of great money in the wedding game, and it can be your new side hustle!

A legal marriage cannot be performed unless you have the state's permission to do so. The restrictions on who can officiate at a wedding are governed by many definitions, categories, and rules that vary from state to state. The simplest option to comply with these requirements is to become ordained with a reputable group that is acknowledged in each of the fifty states.

Once you've chosen where you want to be ordained online, you'll probably apply by completing a form. A printed certificate or minister identification number will be issued to you after your approval. And with that, you are officially ordained.

Once you have the credentials, it's time to find some clients. You'd be smart to reach out to people you already know, offer your services for cheap, and then begin building a collection of previous experience. Get the word out, let others know how easily you work with their plans, and make them feel confident about hiring you for their most special day.

59.
SELL CRAFTS

If you have a natural talent for making things, selling crafts may be a great way for you to make some extra money.

All you need to do is figure out what you want to create, put the time and the effort into making it, and then find a place to sell it. Think of a local arts fair or a flea market or even local shops that sell the work of artists who live near them.

The best thing about making crafts is that it's fun for you and you can charge a pretty penny because they will be handmade. Plus, thanks to websites such as Etsy, you can find potential buyers all over the world. That means that you can almost always find someone to purchase your creations!

60.
AT-HOME CLOTHES CLEANER

When you are an at-home clothes cleaner, you will travel around town and clean other people's clothes for them. You'd be surprised how many people will pay good money for a service like this—that's the modern world we live in!

To begin a side hustle like this, you need to first start by knowing what you're doing. We have all had experience cleaning clothing, but do you have what it takes to do it as a professional side hustle? You will need to buy some supplies and brush up on proper techniques, such as:

- Understanding clothing labels
- Basic stain removal
- How to wash delicate items properly
- Efficient and neat folding techniques

From there, it's probably best to create a post on NextDoor to advertise what you are offering and how much you're asking for a rate. You should start small, like you would with most side hustles. Don't ask for a huge paycheck right as you're getting started because that will come with time.

Pictures, pictures, pictures! Don't forget to create a series of pictures of the work you've done.

61.
FLIP GOODS

Flipping items can be a lucrative and enjoyable side business. Reselling certain products could take some work, but it's worthwhile. You may make a lot of money if you choose the right goods to flip.

The additional money you earn from flipping might build up much more rapidly than you would anticipate. First, get your hands on some common items such as chairs, sofas, tables, and more. Then you'll need to put your own twist on them. Spruce them up, make them look better, or make them look modern and hip.

Once you have done that, hop onto websites such as Amazon, ThredUp, eBay, or Facebook Marketplace and consistently create ads for your work that will catch the attention of people nearby. In no time at all, you can turn this into a side hustle that can pay quite well. Remember, people will pay an arm and a leg for good furniture — you just have to make it for them. Most of these skills are easily learned for free with diligent practice and access to internet videos.

62.
COMPETITIVE GAMER

There is actually a lot of good money in the world of competitive gaming but it's not easy to get into the industry. What are the first steps you need to take if you want to be a competitive gamer?

First, find a game you're really, really good at. Get even better at it. Then, start streaming online like on websites such as YouTube or Twitch to raise awareness of your skills. Build a network of like-minded, similar players and from there you can join a team.

All of this takes a lot of work, and you will end up investing a lot of money in technology to support this side hustle, so keep that in mind if you wish to follow this career path. This is something that you should only try your hand at it if you're already a passionate video game player, otherwise you'll be spending a lot of time and money for nothing.

63.
T-SHIRT DESIGNER

Have you ever had a great idea for a t-shirt and thought you could really sell a few of them? Well, thanks to modern technology, you can make that dream a reality and you can quickly make "t-shirt designer" your new side hustle title.

There are so many great sites out there that can help you turn your t-shirt dreams into reality. You do not need to do it all by hand like the old days. Instead, once you come up with a killer t-shirt idea, turn to sites like Printful, 99designs, Dribble, and more. You will craft your concept and the way it'll look on the shirt and they will do the rest.

Many sites will actually only create the shirts when they are ordered. That means you just need to get the word out about your creations and when someone wants one, the site will print them and ship them. It couldn't be easier.

You need good ideas though! Think about what you see on the market, what's missing, and what you can make. Be very careful to not infringe on someone's trademark. You don't want to get into legal trouble when you are just trying to make a couple extra bucks with your side hustle.

64.
SELL PLASMA

You may know someone who regularly donates blood. But do you know people who donate plasma? In fact, do you even know what plasma is?

Plasma is a production of your blood that's mostly water. However, the rest of its composition is filled with antibodies, enzymes, hormones, and proteins. As you can imagine, it is quite good for our bodies and is in high demand.

And it can be donated, just like blood.

The entire donation process takes just about an hour, and it can pay you very well. You will need to be in good health, between the ages of 18 and 69, weigh at least 110 pounds, and have no infectious diseases, just to name a few criteria.

Many plasma donation centers are willing to pay around $20 to $50 per visit, which you can do every few weeks. And if you plan to be a regular donor, you might get progressively more money upon each visit.

Be sure of two things: you're healthy enough to handle the donation and you're not afraid of needles.

65.
FlexJobs

With a site like FlexJobs, you can find side gigs from all over the country—all over the world in fact—that you can accomplish from the comfort of your own home. The site only allows highly-screened remote jobs that you are free to apply for.

With its constantly growing database, there is a good chance you will find something that calls out to you on FlexJobs. You just need to know what you're looking for and you need to do a great job at pitching yourself to potential employers. Make sure you have a resume handy, and you should also dust off your interview skills because you may be asked to do a virtual interview.

FlexJobs, like UpWork and other freelance sites, is a great way to find any sort of odd job that you think you could really shine at. It's low cost and a really effective way to find that side hustle job that will help you line your pocketbook.

66.
APPJOBS

Like some of the other sites we have listed here, AppJobs is yet another that is perfect for the gig economy and an ideal place to find your next side hustle.

It offers thousands of jobs in more than 600 cities across the United States. The site matches job seekers with businesses that need help, and they will tailor the matches to your specific talents and abilities. They are not a recruitment agency, but they are great at hooking people up to the companies that need specific help.

AppJobs has a lot of jobs ready for you, if you happen to live in one of the cities they cover. Best of all, the site is completely free to use. So, you really have nothing to lose!

67.
SHIFTPIXY

ShiftPixy is an app that helps you find the sort of side hustle gigs that are great for your schedule and your financial needs.

After signing up for the app, you will see a whole slew of jobs nearby that you can apply for. The thing about ShiftPixy is that they make the whole process very easy, and they do a lot of pre-screening before you even apply.

Yes, there is a very uniform and tidy system at play at ShiftPixy. The entire app and process of signing up and applying for jobs is very formal and professional, feels easy, and looks great too.

ShiftPixy takes the entire gig economy to the next level and there is a reason why so many people have signed up to use it. In fact, it sometimes takes a few days after signing up before you can use the app because so many people are jamming into it and trying to find their own side hustles!

Although this app works in a similar manner as other gig economy apps, ShiftPixy connects the gig economy with traditional businesses. It allows applicants to remain in control of their hours and earnings while still allowing them access to medical and retirement benefits.

68.
WONOLO

An extensive employment website called Wonolo predominantly provides entry-level jobs in warehouses and at events, as well as administration. Finding a job with Wonolo is rather easy if you live in one of the cities where they are hooked up. You can simply register, receive daily posts about open positions, and accept the ones that are suitable for you.

At the conclusion of a shift, your employer rates your performance. Your chances of finding more employment increase as your ratings rise and as you take on more jobs. Usually, the worker receives payment five days after an engagement is completed.

The website further exhorts companies to choose their "preferred Wonolers." Due to this, ties between employees and employers can develop over time. When a Wonolo customer hires a Wonolo employee, the customer gives the platform a single, easy payment, and workers receive a portion of that price.

69.
USER INTERVIEWS

A platform for recruitment for market research called User Interviews links researchers with participants who are ready to be a part of their research. You can sign up for the site as a participant to make some additional money if you don't mind taking part in focus groups, research projects, or completing surveys. With this organization, you have the potential to make up to $100 per hour working on some of the top paid research projects currently on the market.

Now, there are many things you might end up doing through User Interviews. You can participate in interviews, focus groups, studies, tasks, and you can even get bonuses each time you refer other people to the company.

There are drawbacks, of course. It takes a while to get your payments so the money will not be in your bank account anytime soon. But if you are good at giving your opinions, then User Interviews might be right for you.

70.
USER TESTING

For a $10 tester fee, User Testing hires independent contractors to evaluate fresh websites and mobile applications. Given that exams last about 20 minutes, this translates to a pleasant hourly salary for a work-from-home position. Tests, however, are not offered every hour or even every day.

The best part about User Testing is that you get paid every week via PayPal, so it's a fast and efficient way to get the money into your bank account as soon as possible.

It's also a lot of fun because you are getting your eyes on first-look sites and apps before they have even hit the market and before other people have seen them. It makes you feel cool and exclusive, like your part of a hip club that is knowledgeable about what's to come.

71.
RECRUITING

Did you know that you can actually get paid to do recruiting work now? Yes, Hired.com will pay you quite well if you do recruiting work on their behalf.

What does it take to recruit? Well, it's pretty much what you imagine. You'll be the one who goes through applications and figures out who's best for a certain job, and you'll also get a cut if they get hired. There are many reasons why this is a great way to make your extra side hustle money. Are you a good judge of character? Do you actually *like* job interviews? Then this might be the right side hustle for you.

72.
FASHION CONSULTANT

Do you love clothes? You may be able to get paid to choose someone's outfit online. Stitch Fix is an online clothes subscription service that assists both men and women in finding stylish attire for special occasions or the workplace.

Users create a profile detailing their own style, after which a stylist is assigned to them who handpicks things they would enjoy wearing. Stylists, who work from home and start off at $15 per hour, are required to have expertise in customer service. Outside of that, this is a good entry-level position for Fashion Consultants.

Make sure to document your progress! Pictures can help you build an online portfolio which will help you connect with clientele who will pay more!

73.
DRONE PILOT

A marketplace platform called DroneBase connects clients in a number of businesses who are looking for aerial solutions with drone operators who can carry out the job. Any pilots with the necessary skillset who are located in a reasonably close geographical region and who submit a project proposal are informed of the opportunity. The position is offered to whichever drone pilot answers first for a predetermined fee.

All the information regarding the location, deadline, necessary type of imagery, anticipated payment amount, and time frame will be sent to you after you register for DroneBase. Once the mission has been completed, you send the photos and filmed product to DroneBase, where they take care of editing and other tasks. Your upload will be examined and paid for after it has been authorized.

74.
PHOTO EDITING

FixThePhoto allows people to go online and have their photography fixed by professionals who are willing to charge far less than many others! Photographers often choose to outsource picture editing services since they spend their time shooting, securing gigs, and promoting. With FixThePhoto, photographers can employ independent contractors to quickly repair their images. On this platform, the photo editors work as independent contractors who often work from home.

To find work, you can promote your editing and retouching rates on the website. You can demand a higher rate than a newcomer in the field if you are able to do a better and more complex job. And you decide your workload! You are free to commit to as many gigs as you like and to work whenever it suits you.

75.
TRANSLATE

Being multilingual does not automatically qualify one to work as a translator. A professional education is necessary to master the particular talent of translation

However, if you are multilingual and have a knack for languages you might want to enroll in a translation program at a recognized college or institution. For beginning translators, several language service providers even provide training programs and credentials, with jobs lined up for anyone who passes a course's final exams.

Working with customers from around the world and learning about various cultures, businesses, and goods are both perks of being a translator. The pay range for translators varies from $20 to $60 per hour based on which languages you speak as well as your area of expertise.

76.
CALL CENTER

When you sign up for a call center job like the ones offered via Liveops, you are basically going to be showing off your customer service skills daily.

That's not a bad thing. This is a great high-paying side hustle that allows you to work from home. You'll need patience, a phone, and an ability to communicate clearly. Liveops, or one of many other call center websites, will teach you everything else you need to know through formal training.

This is a great job for someone who likes to stay indoors and wants to enjoy the summer on their couch while making a little extra money on the side.

77.
CONTACT SERVICE AGENT

Your job as a customer service representative is crucial. You are the face of your business, and it is your responsibility to care for the clients by assisting them with any issues they might be having over the phone or through an online chat. There is no shortage of demand for this position, ranging from technical support to just about any type of help a customer might need.

As a result of the ongoing employment of new representatives by huge tech giants such as Google and Meta, as well as by smaller independent businesses like Nex Rep, there are now more job openings than ever for people who'd like to pursue this career.

78.
LOAN SIGNING AGENT

Have you ever heard of a loan signing agent? You can take classes in your local area to be approved as one. And once you do, you could make some serious green just for getting people to sign on the dotted line.

The main responsibility for a loan signing agent is to sit down with a borrower and ensure that all loan paperwork is correctly completed, notarized, and delivered in a timely manner. Due to the fact that the majority of borrowers work during the day, legal signing agents who are available at odd hours such as evenings are often needed.

So, what is the compensation for this position? A loan signing agent might earn $75 to $125 for each signing appointment. For a full work week, with two after-work visits, you could make as much as $1,000.

79.
MATTRESS FLIPPING

Mattress flipping is a popular side gig that practically anybody can do well. It entails removing furniture from the previous owners, storing the mattresses somewhere clean and dry, and then making a profit from selling the beds to people in the neighborhood.

When customers order mattresses online and then have them shipped, the beds come compressed in a crate to a small portion of their original size.

Even if the consumer wishes to return the product for a refund or replacement, the mattress cannot be placed back in its box after it has been removed from its packaging. Mattress flippers can help in this situation.

Now, obviously you will need a few things if you want to do this job as a side hustle: a truck, a warm and dry place to store the mattresses, and some strength to lift them!

80.
MOVING SERVICES

No one likes moving, but it's a bit easier to handle when you're getting paid very well.

Moving platforms are looking for individuals who can carry 50 to 100 pounds in the spring and summer, peak moving seasons. Although having a vehicle increases your income potential, it is not essential.

Several companies, including GoShare, Truxx, and Laborjack hire movers with or without trucks. If you join GoShare as an employee without a truck, you can make $30 to $45 an hour. Helpers at Truxx make $30 per hour.

Dolly charges $15 an hour for help, and Laborjack pays $15–$20 per hour.

With TaskRabbit, you can set your own pricing and conditions. You can promote your organization and packaging services or work yourself and get paid for your labor. Of course, you can also post your services on NextDoor or Facebook to find your own clients.

81.
MYSTERY SHOPPING

When you sign up as a mystery shopper through companies like Field Agent and BestMark, your job is simple: you have to shop!

You will be told where to go, what to buy, and what to look for. You are essentially giving a business a report card and making sure their products and customer service are top notch. You should only sign up to be a mystery shopper if your attention to detail is strong and you are willing to interact with people.

If you do a good job and agree to multiple mystery shopping assignments, it's possible to receive multiple assignments each month! This can add a lot of money to your bottom line. Plus, you get to paid to go shopping. How fun is that?

82.
IN PERSON
SMALL GIGS

The application process for the secret shopper app Gigwalk is simple. To start earning additional money, just install the app on your phone and provide some verification information. Jobs could include simple tasks like taking photographs of signage or checking to see if a product is offered in a shop. On occasion, asking a cashier if an item is ready and making inquiries about that item might lead to more highly lucrative jobs.

There are, periodically, gigs available only for people who are 21 and older, like checking out alcohol or cigarette items at stores.

People with full-time jobs, students, those wanting to launch a side business, and anybody else looking to make a little more money should check out Gigwalk. Two days after a job is finished, Gigwalk pays via PayPal.

83.
STORAGE SERVICE

When you sign up for a storage service side hustle, you are essentially loaning out the space you own so that other people can keep their possessions safe there.

Now, you'll obviously need a lot of open space, and you must make sure that it's clean, dry, and will not cause any damage to the items that are stored there. This side hustle is perfect for people who have a big garage and would like to make some extra money for keeping things tidy and dry all year long.

A good place to start with this side hustle is the Neighbor storage app. There are many people who need help storing cars, boats, or extra house goods and this app offers an affordable way for them to do that. The app also features insurance options to make sure everyone stays safe and benefits from the transaction.

84.
BECOME A
MOVIE EXTRA

Are you ready for your close up?

If you live in a part of the country where movies are filmed, you may be in luck if you have the time to be a movie extra.

First of all, this will only work if you live in a location where movies are being created. If that's the case, you should hop online to one of the many sites that look for extras, like Craigslist, Facebook, and Backstage West. Central Casting is one of the more well-known casting agencies out there. Finding a casting agent will increase your opportunities and chances of being hired. Remember that movies are often looking for people with a certain type of looks, so not everyone is going to get a part.

When you're an extra, you'll be sitting around most of the day. But you'll get paid quite well for the long wait. Plus, you might see a few celebrities!

85.
LOOK AT THINGS
ON EBAY

WeGoLook pays independent contractors to examine vehicles, locations, properties, and establishments. After signing up for the site, a description of a task that includes the compensation, the location, and the requirements will be sent to you. The task is then up to you, and you need to give honest feedback about it.

If you accept the position, you must finish the work in just one day. Driving to the location, snapping several photos, and commenting on various information will all be required for this job.

The average length of time required for a job with WeGoLook is just about half an hour; therefore, the price of up to $30 per task seems fair. Yet, independent contractors claim that they are frequently required to make costly long-distance trips. Nevertheless, there is no requirement to accept offers. So, if you ignore long-distance or time-consuming offers, you ought to be able to earn minimum wage or more. Payment is made within 30 days after the conclusion of the examination. The quantity of individuals WeGoLook has nearby affects your chances of finding jobs with this app, so it's not ideal for people living in rural communities.

86.
CREATE PSYCHIC READINGS

Your phone or tablet will receive customized psychic readings directly from Purple Ocean. You could try to ask questions about money, marriage, and destiny with this ground-breaking service and receive video answers right away using iOS or Android app.

If you register using the app, you can become one of those mediums. If you don't have a strong understanding of what you're doing as well as something unique to offer the customers, this will be a waste of your time. This kind of work is only recommended for those with prior knowledge and practice as a medium.

Once you sign up, you'll want to extensively promote the app on all of your social media platforms. If you want to make a true living from this side gig, you need a lot of visitors to your page. Some mediums do this by creating videos on YouTube and social media to promote their services.

87.
SELL TAROT
CARD READINGS

If you have a talent for tarot card reading then you should join the countless professionals who have made a side hustle career for themselves online doing just that.

Thanks to Facebook, Fiverr, and Instagram, you can attract people to your profile and your skills. You'll need to know how to read tarot cards and you'll need some people to give testimonies on your behalf, so others believe that you're the real deal.

Tarot card reading has become even more popular over the last few years. It is vital that you do a good job and remain personable and friendly throughout every reading. You can charge upwards of $40 per reading, so your clients need to get some serious bang for their buck. Many readers will create general readings and offer them up for free on YouTube and then offer extended and personal readings for purchase on Vimeo.

88.
TALK TO
PEOPLE ONLINE

Some people just want companionship. And you can give it to them as a side hustle thanks to the internet.

You can create a profile on Instagram, Fiverr, YouTube, or other sites where you quite frankly just speak your mind. And people will listen! And they will even pay to hear your opinions and your voice on certain subjects. TikTok is another platform where you can do this, as well as Patreon.

You'll need to perfect your public speaking skills and focus on creating powerful content that brings people back again and again. But there are millions of people making a pretty penny by just talking and speaking their minds. Start with the subject you are most passionate about.

89.
CORPORATE GIFT
CONSULTANT

There are tons of platforms that offer corporate gift giving consultations to help corporations choose and give gifts to everyone from employees who resign to new customers.

There are plenty of companies that need help when it comes to figuring out what to buy for people. This is due to the growing significance of providing the appropriate present to suppliers, business partners, and clients.

You can operate this interesting side business entirely online or in person. To increase and complement your income throughout the holidays, take corporate gift consulting into consideration. This is a great job for anyone who loves the winter season and buying gifts for family and friends. It will require research and some work to build a client list, though.

Here are some tips for getting started:

- Start by reaching out to local companies.
- Find companies with large client and employee numbers (think real estate and franchise).
- Talk directly to HR managers about the service you can provide.
- Be willing to deliver the gifts directly to the clientele or employees.

90.
PUBLIC SPEAKING COACH

Did you know that a lot of people are terrified of public speaking? In fact, there are many people who would do just about anything to avoid speaking in public! It's a true fear.

But if you are good at public speaking, there are people who are willing to pay good money to learn the tricks of the trade and overcome their anxiety. You will have to make sure you really know what you're talking about. Plus, you'll also need to be able to convey your opinions and knowledge with ease.

Craigslist and Facebook are great to start advertising your coaching skills. Also, any place associated with a college is a good place to start. There are always students who need help with public speaking.

91.
HOLIDAY ERRAND SERVICE

The holidays are a very busy time and not everyone has the ability to do everything on their lists. That's why you should try being a holiday errand service specialist as a side hustle.

It's really quite easy. You'll simply do the jobs that no one else has time for. You pick up — or wrap — gifts. You drop things off. You make reservations. It's a lot like being a personal assistant but it's specifically about that holly, jolly time of the year. A good place to start is with your neighbors. Post listings on Craigslist, Facebook, NextDoor, and other forms of social media.

92.
DATING CONSULTANT

Some people are just unlucky in love — but you can help them with that. For a fee, of course.

Being a dating consultant is a service you can advertise on sites like Fiverr. Basically, you will be helping people put together their dating website profiles, and determining what it is they are looking for. You will also give them pointers about dating — how to dress, where to go, how to act, and what to ask.

Dating is really hard. Everyone knows that. But everyone also *wants* to date, even if they're a bit fearful. Becoming a dating consultant is a great way for you to help others in need and bring a bit of joy—and romance—into someone's life.

93.
HOME FILMING LOCATION

If there are movies or TV shows being filmed in your town, you should really offer up your house as a possible filming location for them.

You can get paid—a lot—when you sign up to do this. However, it's not a sure thing, even if you have a great house. You need to remember that each production is looking for very specific things, from the way the house is laid out, to the year it was built, to the amount of space it has.

But if your home *is* selected you can pretty much rest assured that your mortgage will be taken care of for a few months.

94.
PROCESS SERVER

Legally, process servers must follow their state's guidelines while serving documents on behalf of the courts. State rules will vary; however, it is feasible for you to work as a process server in your free time provided you are an adult, have never been found guilty of a crime, and are able to interact with strangers in a courteous manner.

If you don't mind interacting directly with folks who are dealing with legal problems, this is a terrific method for you to earn some additional cash. Always maintain a professional demeanor! And perhaps be prepared for the unexpected as well. Start this side hustle by researching your local requirements and filling out the necessary paperwork at the county clerk offices.

95.
VISUAL MERCHANDISER

There is a rhyme and reason to the way that every single store is laid out and that's all due to visual merchandisers. In-store displays are managed by a visual merchandiser. When you pursue this side hustle, you create the external and interior displays for the business in order to present goods with the ideal style and appearance that will encourage customers to make purchases. You are in charge of selecting and putting up the display's backdrop and items, and making sure storefront windows are captivating and consistent with the store's brand.

It helps to have a background in design and marketing as well as retail job experience if you wish to become a visual merchandiser. Some positions require an associate degree, but there are many small businesses that need help from entry-level designers. To develop the necessary skills for this vocation, you should study design, advertising, and color theory.

96.
SENIOR CITIZEN DOWNSIZING SERVICES

To simplify daily life, downsizing involves clearing out clutter and relocating into a smaller house. Experts in downsizing houses are usually on hand to help with chores like clearing, arranging, moving, and packing in order to make this process go as easily and simply as possible.

You can do this for elderly people who want to downsize their living space or who want to move into a retirement community. Some people may want to sell their old items on eBay, while others may want to donate them to community centers or gift them to family members. Having a truck, cleaning and packing supplies, and basic knowledge of reselling items is a good strategy before getting started.

This job calls for a lot of love, patience, care, and awareness of the unique circumstances these elderly individuals are facing. There are many that need help. Always treat them with care, as well as their belongings. One way to find clients is by alerting front desk workers at Senior Citizen homes and retirement communities about the services you're offering.

97.
UI/UX TESTER

UI/UX testing is a side hustle that allows you to try out a website, report back on what works and doesn't work, and lets you get paid well while doing so.

To do this job, you'll need to make sure you have a strong internet connection and also a valid PayPal account. You may also need to download an extension and some social media accounts.

It usually only takes around 30 minutes to complete a typical UI/UX test. You will need to pay close attention to the most minute details and be able to report back what you find very plainly and accurately.

98.
DATA ENTRY

Since working from home has surged in popularity, so have data entry positions. All you need is an internet connection, some data to enter, and an understanding of the applications required by the company.

This can be a monotonous job. So, you'll want to have something to keep you engaged. Maybe you can listen to a book on tape or have music playing at all times. Or maybe you'll want to take a lot of breaks. It's important that all the data is entered accurately every single time, without exception.

You can't make many mistakes when you are doing data entry, but you can do it from your home, even from your couch or bed. It doesn't get much better than that! Data entry jobs can be easily found on freelance websites or through a quick search online.

99.
RECOVER UNCLAIMED PROPERTY

Annually, states return unclaimed property worth billions of dollars. Unrecovered cash in bank and financial accounts that have remained untouched for longer than a year is often considered to be unclaimed assets.

Since the federal government does not maintain a centralized website for locating unclaimed property, the procedure for recovering abandoned property differs by state. Many state websites follow a similar pattern and are usually not too difficult to use. The official organization in charge of maintaining the inventory of unclaimed property is often the department of the local comptroller.

California is one of the simpler states since you can obtain their list of debtors and utilize free online resources to find out who owes money. Then, if you assist them in completing the paperwork, you will be compensated with 10% of the entire amount.

100.
CRYPTO MINING

You might not know a lot about cryptocurrency, but you should know that it needs to be "mined". What does that mean exactly? It means that a computer composed simply for mining is created and will constantly be descrambling a complex, ever-changing code to create a brand new "block" of crypto.

It's all very complicated but the bottom line is that crypto mining is a great way to make money as a side hustle. All you have to do is create the computer necessary to do it. That is quite the task, and it will require a lot of research, energy, and money. But it will be well worth it because if your computer does mine some crypto, it could be worth tens of thousands of dollars.

There are many tutorials online about how to create a "mining rig" that you will need to get your crypto. Keep in mind that this won't be a short and simple task. Prepare to spend a lot, tweak it a lot, and then wait a lot. But all you need is one good mining experience to make it well worth your time and money!

101.
SOCIAL MEDIA
ADVERTISING

If you are aware of social media and influencers, then you are already aware of the world of social media advertising. When you work as a social media advertiser, you will have to keep up with all the trends and be aware of everything that is happening in your area of expertise. Instead of working for a brand, you are working as the brand. If you are going to be at the forefront of advertising, your face and who you are will likely be connected to the industry you are pushing.

To start working in social media advertising, you will need to develop some skills to make sure you remain a strong business. Get some practice in accounting, profit trends, social media legal practices, and obviously—technology. Working in social media advertising means that you are your own business and choose your own hours. You also have control over which industry you follow or if you want to advertise on a more general scale. It's important to know what your "brand" will be before you get too far into it. People generally don't like it when advertisers switch up what they are doing too often.

Social media advertising is a great side hustle because you can do it from your own home, on your own time, and from your phone. Take time to get your agency properly set up so you don't have any financial loss or legal troubles. Hey, we already spend so much time on social media, so why not make it your side hustle?

CONCLUSION

In this day and age, there are endless ways to make extra money from home — all you have to do is start! This book is only a beginning guide to help give you ideas. It is up to you to take action and find what works best for you!

As long as you are honest about your skill level, there are many opportunities for people without any experience in these fields. Take a moment to think about what resources you have and what you are good at, then choose a few of these side hustles to get you started. Who knows, within a few short months, your side gig could transform into a full-fledged career! You'll never know until you give it a shot.

Printed in Great Britain
by Amazon

55353808R00079